PHOEBE DARQUELING
The Steampunk Handbook

First published by Tainted Tincture Press 2020

Copyright © 2020 by Phoebe Darqueling

All rights reserved. No part of this publication may be reproduced, stored or transmitted in any form or by any means, electronic, mechanical, photocopying, recording, scanning, or otherwise without written permission from the publisher. It is illegal to copy this book, post it to a website, or distribute it by any other means without permission.

Phoebe Darqueling asserts the moral right to be identified as the author of this work.

Phoebe Darqueling has no responsibility for the persistence or accuracy of URLs for external or third-party Internet Websites referred to in this publication and does not guarantee that any content on such Websites is, or will remain, accurate or appropriate.

First edition

ISBN: 978-1-7347298-0-1

Cover art by P.R. Chase

This book was professionally typeset on Reedsy.
Find out more at reedsy.com

The Steampunk Handbook

By Phoebe Darqueling

— ARTWORK BY —
P. R. CHASE

Table of Contents

Foreword - 1

Where's the Steam? A Brief History of Steam Power - 4

Where's the Punk? The Etymology of "Punk" - 14

The Roots of Steampunk - Steampunk before "Steampunk" - 27
   The First Decade: 1987-1996 - 37
   The Second Decade: 1997-2006 - 44
   The Third Decade: 2007 to the present - 59

12 Popular Tropes in Steampunk: AKA Ways to Punk Your Steam - 77
   Make it Alien - 80
   Make it Alternative - 87
   Make it Feminist - 96
   Make it Funny - 105
   Make it Futuristic - 116
   Make it Multi-Cultural - 121
   Make it Musical - 129
   Make it Playable - 135
   Make it Scary - 142
   Make it Supernatural - 157

Make it Travel Through Time - 178
Make it Yours - 190

A Few Parting Thoughts - 197

Read More From Phoebe Darqueling: Riftmaker

Read More from Phoebe Darqueling: Mistress of None Series

Edited by Phoebe Darqueling

About the Illustrator

Foreword

If you aren't familiar with what "Steampunk" means, here's a brief definition: It began as a literary genre loosely inspired by the real or imagined cultures, events, and technologies of the Industrial and Victorian eras (roughly speaking, the 19th century but there's wiggle room). Steampunk can take various forms, from an alternative history to a dystopian future to a complete fantasy world untethered to our sense of time and space. In the over thirty years since the rather tongue-in-cheek coining of the word, Steampunk has leaped from the pages of books and into people's lives in the form of special events, elaborate costumes, and dedicated "sports."

The primary goal of *The Steampunk Handbook* is to facilitate that inspiration and provide some food for thought, as well as resources, to get your gears going. The rest of this book is basically devoted to expanding on and explaining the brief definition above, so if you are still having trouble wrapping your head around it, don't worry. I know that some people will read it straight through, while others will be more interested in particular chapters. For this reason, you may see some examples and ideas repeated to ensure that however someone wants to use this resource, they get the full picture.

The first two chapters are devoted to understanding "steam," understanding "punk," and understanding the history of punk literature. This is followed by four chapters that look at specific works and how the fandom has expanded, starting with the literary underpinnings of the genre and going through the distinct steps that have brought us to where we are today.

I've been an active member of the Steampunk community as a blogger, an author, and a lecturer since 2013, and I continue to be delighted by this fandom. I wholeheartedly believe that anyone who wants to participate can and should be able to do so, even if funds are limited and time is short.

For that reason, I do not claim that this little handbook is comprehensive. Inevitably, things had to be left out in order to keep it both inexpensive and compact for the consumer. It is certainly biased toward the things I find personally interesting, and the conclusions are biased by my experiences. I am not trying to compete with the likes of beautiful *Steampunk Bible*, which is chock-full of images that demonstrate the aesthetic that I only refer to in these pages. My hope is to provide a jumping off point for understanding the evolution of the genre, to guide you to a sampling of the works across various media that have been involved so far, and provide information to help you go off and create something splendid of your own.

"Phoebe Darqueling" is a pen name (pronounced like "darkling"), but in my real life, I studied anthropology and art history at a liberal arts college. I am currently the Creative Director for a creativity competition for kids and I edit academic works by non-native English speakers. Though I have lived in a few different European countries, the majority of my experiences are within the American Steampunk community. These experiences have shaped my approach to understanding this micro-culture, as well as the history that underpins it.

The majority of this book is devoted to "Ways to Punk Your Steam," which reflects the patterns I have observed. These are twelve tropes you can find within Steampunk, as well as some reference material recommendations and explanations of the historical context for each. These are by no means the *only* tropes; they are simply the ones that I observed and was interested enough in to do further research.

No doubt, some people will feel that I cast my net too wide, that I am too inclusive. But this is who I am, and this is my contribution to the conversation. I hope it inspires you to add your voice as well.

Chapter 2

Where's the Steam?

More than likely, you've encountered mentions of steam-based technology at some point in your life. Museums often have displays about locomotives or Industrial era machines from factories. Starting in the 1750s, the Western world began to embrace the power of steam, and it fundamentally changed their place on the global scale in the 1800s. So, it makes sense to equate this technology with that era. However, steam power is a very old and diverse way to accomplish all kinds of goals. Here are a few examples from history.

1st Century C.E.

The "aeolipile," AKA "Hero's engine" is a precursor to the complex steam-powered turbines used in Victorian era factories. It gets its name from Aeolus, the Greek god of wind. There is a chamber, usually spherical, that is full of water. The escaping steam causes the chamber to spin, creating torque. The illustration below is based on Hero's description of encountering the device in Roman Egypt. It wasn't very powerful or put to much use, but it is an early example of creating movement using steam power.

1125 C.E.

Historian William of Malmesbury first described a musical organ powered by heating water. Many centuries later, the first calliope design was patented and also ran on steam power. Circuses and steamships used steam- and gas-powered organs like these because the sound reached for several miles and announced their arrival to the masses. Starting in 1859, the technology was improved by Arthur S. Denny, who demonstrated a quieter, more easily controlled calliope at the Crystal Palace.

1601 C.E.

Giovanni Battista della Porta built a series of fountains using steam power to create a vacuum to propel the water through the pipes. This is the precursor to percolators like those employed in coffee makers designed by physicist Benjamin Thompson in the 1810s.

1698 C.E.

Thomas Savery created the "Miner's Friend," though many speculate it was a copy of a design created by Edward Somerset, who did not live long enough to see the concept implemented. In both cases, cold water or additional vapor is introduced into the system to increase the vacuum pressure. The purpose was to pump water great distances out of mining operations. However, many mine owners worried about the intense pressures being reached, and it wasn't until nearly a century later that the design was used on a large scale.

1705 C.E.

Thomas Newcomen further improved engine designs by introducing the use of pistons. His design was like Savery's in many ways, so Necomen, his partner John Calley, and Savery often exhibited their inventions together and cooperatively. By 1718, Jean Desguliers improved on the design to offer safety valves to decrease the danger of explosion under pressure. After Newcomen's patent expired in 1733, many more of his style of engines were built and eventually spread to what would become the United States of America.

1765 C.E.

James Watt made the next big improvement on the steam engine by adding another chamber for the condensing water. In earlier models, the engine would cool with every stroke, but his version allowed more of the preheated water to return to the boiler. This meant it took less time and energy to heat it up again and greatly improved efficiency. However, in practice he was unable to create a good enough seal around his pistons due to the type of cylinder he could produce, and the machine didn't perform well at first. It took ten more years after the patent was issued (1769) before he was able to get a sufficient seal to prove how much better his idea was than previous designs.

What About Asia?

Despite the fact that ancient empires like China and Japan made other types of scientific advancements, steam power was slow to spread into Asia. There are many different theories surrounding what many refer to as "The Great Divergence." So many different theories exist that I won't attempt to delve into them here. But it is easy to see that some combination of factors in Western Europe, and especially Great Britain, led to the innovations that shaped the steam era.

The Industrial Revolution

Over the next century, several great minds would make refinements on steam engines to allow them to be used in textile mills and other types of factories. For a long time, every single engine had to be built completely from scratch with one-of-a-kind parts. This made both mistakes and maintenance sometimes difficult and costly. The next big leap forward occurred when people started to create factories to create other machines rather than finished products. Once the specifications for a particular patent were established, more engines could be created. For a long time, trained people were still necessary to carry out the work, but the codifying of the size and shapes of various parts facilitated the spread of steam into more contexts.

For a firsthand experience of some of these marvelous machines, I highly recommend the Museum of Water and

Steam in London. They have a collection of beautiful and still-functioning engines on a large scale.

The implications of steam power are far wider than just the industries they helped to grow. It also brought about far-reaching social changes as well. By making production more efficient, the cost of goods began to drop. Cloth, for instance, could be purchased and turned into clothes much more cheaply than before. This was bad for the people who had been producing small-scale textiles in their homes, but it was good for general health. In a world where people rarely bathed because they worried about the bad smells getting in, people suddenly started to be able to change their clothes more regularly. And when you can choose your clothes, clothes start to become important to a greater number of people. Fashion was no longer just something that the great lords and ladies thought about, it was something that differentiated the haves and have-nots across a much wider spectrum.

The new steam-powered factories and the people who manufactured parts for them attracted workers to cities. The demand for housing, food, and other commodities grew, often outstripping a city's ability to provide them. The immigrants were just as likely to find slums and squalor as they were to find work. And as soon as you had more people piled on top of one another and fewer resources to go around, crime became the way of life for many.

Factories also allowed for reading material to be created at a faster rate than ever before. Paper mills, book printers, book binders—they all benefited from steam power and other technological advancements that went hand in hand with it. And as people flocked to cities and literacy rates increased, the demand for stories skyrocketed.

CHAPTER 2

Steam Transportation

Another side effect of harnessing steam power was that people started to become more mobile than before. Locomotives provided a way to move goods and people around a country or between countries at an unprecedented rate. The first steam-powered locomotive started operating in 1804, but the first commercially viable one wasn't developed until around 1812 by John Blenkinsop. The first locomotive to carry passengers appeared in 1825.

In addition to taking people into the city to look for work and crops into the city to feed them, locomotives also opened up the world for tourism. Beach resorts and other vacation spots started to pop up around this time, and people could go out to neighboring towns to attend their local festivals or a traveling show and be back in time for supper.

Depending on the tides and winds to control a sailing ship left a lot of room for error, and the threat of simply drifting on a becalmed sea until your food ran out was ever-present. A steam ship, on the other hand, could keep chugging along whether or not there was a breeze to power it. This meant that not only were fewer ships lost, but merchants could also depend on their cargoes arriving by a certain date. This in turn allowed stores to be able to guarantee their stock of goods. All around, steam power helped to bring stability and security to trade done on waterways.

In addition, new products could be offered. For instance, ice was a commodity that required fast transport, often from the frozen lakes of North America all the way across the ocean at a time when there were no electric freezers. In other places, new raw materials could be transported to faraway factories, then the finished goods were widely dispersed. The ability to move products such as silk from the East to the West created a market for these goods and an interest in foreign countries and cultures.

Steam ships built for both the ocean and rivers also had an effect on how wars were waged. Controlling traffic on and across the Mississippi River was a major concern during the American Civil War. Japan, which had successfully repelled Western influence for centuries, was forced to open their borders when a flotilla of armed and armored vessels came to their shores.

Not long after steam technology was applied to travel, it also found its way into farm equipment. Farmers could cultivate more land and harvest more crops. This meant that there was more food at a lower price, but it also fed into the influx of people leaving the countryside in search of jobs in the city.

Alternatives to Steam Power

Depending on who you ask, the use of steam power can be what defines a Steampunk story, or it is simply a reference to a rough time period and the social issues that arose as a result of a leap in technological advancement. Here are a few other types of technology you can find in Steampunk stories that have little to do with actual steam.

Electricity

Steampunk often falls into the realm of alternative history, and the world would have looked very different if electricity had become the norm rather than steam power during the 19th century. The needs and limitations of first using wood, then coal, to power steam factories shaped the nature of both cities and the countryside.

CHAPTER 2

Some people go so far as to classify alternative history that uses electricity as its own "punk" genre. "Teslapunk" is named, of course, for the great and eccentric scientist, Nikola Tesla. He was an Armenian immigrant working for Thomas Edison, and their falling out is the stuff of steam era legend. The line between Steampunk and Teslapunk is very blurry because Tesla himself makes regular appearances in Steampunk media.

Aether

I attended a lecture at the International Steampunk Symposium in 2016 by "Zebulon Vitruvius Pike" that did a wonderful job of outlining the "science" of aether. I used his information as well as my own further research to create a lecture called "Of Aether and Alchemy" that I delivered at the same event in 2017.

The understanding of aether in the steam era and the way it is applied in Steampunk often differ. (On a side note, when spelled like "ether" instead, it most often refers to the gas breathed as either an anesthesia or an intoxicant, but it is also a valid spelling.) The word dates way back to Aristotle, who theorized that the world was made up of four elements (fire, water, earth, and air) and something existing outside of them called aether. It held none of the properties of the other elements. Instead, it was like the "glue" that held everything together. He also believed this was what the gods breathed because in his worldview, it existed "above" the air.

In the 17th century, people started to take this philosophical notion out of the mind and into practice. Renee Descartes (of "I think, therefore I am" fame) rejected the idea that objects could influence one another across a vacuum (AKA motion at a distance). Instead, Descartes believed there had to be some kind of medium in between to transmit vibrations, and he called this medium aether. He viewed gravity as a pushing force rather than a pulling force as we most often think of it today. He envisioned whirlpools of "gravitational aether" spiraling around heavy bodies, such as the Sun, and pushing the planets along before it.

The other type of aether was called "luminiferous aether," meaning "light-bearing aether." Much like gravitational aether, luminiferous aether was an attempt to explain how light (and other electromagnetic phenomena) could move from one place to another. Though many experiments were conducted to try to prove both types of aether existed, none were ever a success. By the time Einstein was publishing his theories aether had more less fallen completely out of favor by the scientific community.

In Sir Arthur Conan Doyle's novel, *The Poison Belt*, aether is portrayed as being like big invisible clouds moving around the universe. Some of these clouds were toxic to life, and as one passed through the same area of space as the Earth, the entire population lay down where they stood. Luckily for the human race, it eventually passed and everyone got up and went about their lives as if nothing had happened.

In Steampunk fiction, many people swap in aether as an alternative to, but functioning exactly like, electricity. Oftentimes, some kind of crystal is employed to gather or focus this energy source into a laser-like weapon. This is not very much like what scientists who studied aether believed, but it does result in some fun props and costumes with bits lighting up. Other times, aether is treated as a sort of wind power that can be caught by specialized sails and used to propel airships.

A New Substance

In some cases, Steampunk worlds are powered by something completely new to "science." Often, this is something mined out of the earth, like H.G. Wells' "cavorite" that was "opaque to gravity" and allowed for a voyage to the moon. It might be something that allows good, old-fashioned steam engines to run more efficiently, or replace them altogether. Usually, it isn't radioactive in the sense that it can cause mutation, but it may be like plutonium or radium in that it puts off heat or light of its own.

It could also take the form of a gas that fills airship envelopes or can be burned. If it looks or acts like fossil fuel, then you start to get into Dieselpunk territory, but depending on the other trappings in the fictional society, it could be possible to see an internal combustion engine using a made-up substance in a Steampunk story. Other times, it is extraterrestrial in origin or created by alchemists in a lab rather than mined. And depending on how much the creator leans either toward science fiction or fantasy, this new mystery substance could simply be equated with magic.

No matter what people use to power their Steampunk worlds, using the impact of technology on the 19th century world as the jumping off point is at its core. The types of social and other wide-reaching issues that snowballed from harnessing this energy source is what matters more than the actual heating of water and turning of axles. So, that takes care of the "steam" part of the term. But what about the punk?

Chapter 3

I decided to write the article this chapter is based on after I saw the question of "where is the PUNK in Steampunk, anyway?" come up in a thread on the _United we Steampunk, Divided we Fall_ group I run on Facebook. It's a fun place to connect with your fellow Steampunk fans, and I invite you to join us for discussions, sharing, and general splendidness.

The Philosophical Roots of Punk

I was born in 1984, so I spent a large portion of the late

punk era watching Saturday morning cartoons. This is around the same time the word Steampunk came into being. So, it seems like the right moment in time to begin the discussion of the word "punk" and how it has changed since then. I am too young to pretend to be an expert in punk through experience, but there is a lot to learn through research.

When the punk movement began in the 1970s, there were a few important pieces at its heart. One was an anti-establishment ethos. You don't have to be an anarchist, but good punks rebel against how "the system" works against the people rather than for them. Punks oppose those systems and the people who propagate them by acting and dressing in a way that disturbs people and rocks them out of the status quo. There's an undeniable element of theatricality as these limits (and the accompanying mohawks) got pushed bigger and wider. At its heart, "punk" seeks to make people question the idea of "normal" and those institutions that strive to establish a single right answer.

Punk clothing was a direct and conscious breaking with the mainstream fashions. Individual expression became paramount. (Though, of course, even this became codified to some degree, much to the chagrin of the "true" punks. Sound familiar...?) Another example of this would be the grunge movement, which emerged around the same time punk was fading. In both cases, the wearers were pushing against a stiff formality and the dictates of what was proper for them to wear.

Ironically, as casual attire has become the norm, many contemporary punks have swung in the other direction. Many people lament how "slovenly" and sloppy our expectations have become and feel nostalgia for a buttoned-up past. And this isn't just about clothes. As our culture has become more egalitarian, we've also lost the emphasis on good manners and formal speech.

This isn't to say that an egalitarian society breeds mean people, but when there is a conscious shift away from mimicking the codes and folkways of the upper classes in order to illustrate the new emphasis on being equal, many of these "niceties" have fallen away completely. Nobody in the English-speaking world bows, for instance. We don't have strict protocols regarding who you are allowed to touch with your ungloved hand. There are fewer ways to show respect to one's "betters" when a culture has worked to do away with the notion.

Take your average American teenager, for example. It's not uncommon for a young person to make a conscious shift in how they address their parents and the level of respect they outwardly display. This is a stage in many people's process of identity-building. And as our highly connected world culture has continued to mature, this has translated in a general movement away from the formal trappings of etiquette in the Western world.

While striving for equality is certainly better than the alternative, this casualness can and often does swing too far. Certain segments of the Internet are now a wasteland full of angry trolls and hateful words. Though the pressure to use or abandon specific words that refer to different groups can certainly be viewed as a new step on the road to politeness, it is also easier than ever to find people who specifically push back against "political correctness" and band together to do so. Many Anachropunks see the way people treat each other now as something that needs to stop, and deliberately choosing things from the past to revive as the way to combat it. Steampunks especially embrace the idea of "being splendid."

CHAPTER 3

This applies to dressing fabulously, but also to being kind and conscious of the implications our costume and other choices can have on those around us.

The punk attitudes about conformity dovetails with the belief that no one should be able to tell you how to act and, by extension, interact with the things you love. Punk musicians didn't play music because they were prodigies. They did it because they wanted to express themselves through music. In the same way, Anachropunk writers, makers, and cosplayers are doing the same thing and interacting with the eras that inspire them.

However, this can also make it hard to strike the right balance of being punk and being splendid. As I was putting the final touches on this book, I attended TeslaCon 9. I am a member of the associated Facebook groups, and in the weeks following the event, someone started a thread asking that people refrain from wearing Shriner's official fezzes as part of their apparel. I was not aware, but it turns out that donating, buying, or selling a Shriner fez is a big no-no within the organization. Much to my surprise, this comment thread exploded with responses ranging from the realm of "I'm so sorry, I had no idea that would offend someone" to "Grow up and stop complaining." Not only defining Steampunk, but defining what "being splendid" in the Steampunk community is, continues to be a moving target.

> "I THINK PART OF THE REASON [STEAMPUNK] REALLY IS PUNK
> IS THAT IT HAS THAT WONDERFUL PUNK ETHOS,
> OF YOU DO IT BY DOING IT. AND ANYBODY CAN DO IT.
> IT ACTUALLY SEEMS TO BE ABOUT A
> LIFESTYLE FOR SOME PEOPLE.
> IT'S ABOUT SO MUCH MORE THAN
> BRASS GOGGLES
> AS A FASHION STATEMENT."
>
> -NEIL GAIMAN

Oftentimes, dissatisfaction of punks about the status quo showed through the music and other creations. The ethos led to action (as well as many, many mosh pits), and even in the early days, "punk" was synonymous with "doing." These might not have always been actions the mainstream *liked* (and by definition, that was pretty much the point), which further tweaked the meaning.

During the 1990s, the noun got verbed and came to mean something like "taking action in order to cause mischief." Pretty soon, farmers everywhere were shaking their sawed-offs at passersby yelling, "Stay off my lawn, you punks!"

Later, if a person had mischief done onto them, you could say they "had been punked." This made them a punk, but confusingly, the person who did the mischief could also be considered a punk.

By 2003, this shift was so popular, MTV named its celebrity prank program "Punk'd." The host made a variety of famous people the butt of a joke, both humanizing our idols (the status quo) and cementing the meaning as a verb. Plus, dropping the "e" is punking the very spelling of the word punked. Nice one, MTV.

CHAPTER 3

Punk Literature

It all started with Cyberpunk. In 1980, writer Bruce Bethke wrote a story with that title by combining "cybernetics," the science of replacing human functions with computerized ones, and "punk," as discussed in this chapter. Though cybernetics itself was a term coined in the 1940s, the big wave of research occurred in the 1970s and 80s, making it a quintessential technology for that time period. From there, other people started using this naming convention to coin many new literary genres.

The Anachropunk sub-genres all have punk values at their core. And it's why I keep coming back for more. Maybe I'm odd because I love them all, maybe I'm not. Make no mistake; I am not drawing a direct, causal line between mohawks and tea-dueling. Instead, the goal of this chapter is to highlight where I see the overlap between the principles and co-evolution of the words punk and Steampunk, as well as the other "punks" that have come about since.

Some people prefer "Metapunk," "Retropunk," or other terms to mean the same thing I do with Anachropunk. I just like the sound of it, and it carries slightly different connotations than the others. Plus, it feels like a word with enough room to include a lot of works by different people in different fandoms.

The beginning of the word — "anachro" — means roughly "without regard to time." You have probably seen the word "anachronism" before, meaning a phrase or object in the wrong time period. This could be something annoying like slang from the 1920s being used in a film set in 1890. On the other hand, anachronisms can be downright hilarious. The thing that matters is the juxtaposition. By putting two things together that don't belong, it calls attention to both. This is why we love mash-ups so much!

When "anachro" is combined with "punk," you get a word that means "giving the finger to 'the man' without regards to time period." For writers, 'the man' could be the mainstream publishing house that won't buy your amazing crossover fiction because they don't think it would sell. "The man" could be your employer who won't let you dress in your fancy duds whenever you want. We are all faced with people and institutions that thrive on telling us "no." Punks don't take no for an answer. Instead, they keep on asking, "What if?"

Schisms and Common Ground

The term "Cyberpunk" may have come first, but since the 1908s, the number of different subgenres has skyrocketed. There is ample room for overlap depending on your parameters, and occasionally a writer or reviewer will attempt to coin a new subgenre moniker for a single crossover work, thus muddying the waters. Sometimes, these fans and creators are sequestering themselves by strict time guidelines. Others are only interested in the corresponding technology. There's Atompunk (roughly early days of space travel), Silkpunk (various parts of Asian history), Afropunk (the experience of Africans and their diaspora)—just to name a few. These are all direct off-shoots of the notion of the punk ethos of questioning authority and honoring misfits, just set in different times, cultural contexts, and places.

This in-group, out-group gnashing of teeth plays out all over the Internet, and the various Anachropunk communities are no different. I tend to be a "lumper" rather than a "splitter," so I wanted a word that would cover all of these amazing punks regardless of which time period inspires them.

Others like to split. "Clockpunk" precedes Steampunk in time, focusing on the Renaissance and the age before steam power became prevalent (though airships do make an appearance). This is distinct from "Gearpunk," which I have seen defined as applying Steampunk aesthetics to something without the historical underpinning driving the act (such as the much-maligned practice of "just glue some gears on it"), but also as a term totally interchangeable with Steampunk and being 100% the same. Dieselpunk is probably the most well-established punk after Cyber and Steam, and is basically the World War eras. However, nestled *within* Diesel is "Decopunk," which focuses specifically on the 1920s (give or take a couple of years). You can also punk the future if you want, using Biopunk and Solarpunk, depending on the technology applied. In general, Solarpunk tends to be more optimistic about the future than any of the others.

Personally, I tend to think of Gaslamp Fantasy and Steampunk as being part of the same continuum even though the word punk doesn't appear in the former. However, only their approach to messing with the past varies, but usually not the specific time associated with Steampunk. In many ways, Steampunk is the science fiction side and Gaslamp is the fantasy side to the same coin, especially because of the varying degrees of liberties writers take with what "science" means.

However, I know many people care about these distinctions, and some very deeply. That's fine, too. We can both enjoy the things we love in our own way. It's part of what makes us punks.

Punking the Past to Talk about the Present

Just because someone uses the trappings of the past to inform their setting, it doesn't limit their messages to topics in the past. Steampunk stories often use an Industrial era setting in order to explore contemporary issues. The way humans evolve alongside the technology they create is at the heart of much of speculative fiction.

This historical flavor of the "what if" game isn't the sole provenance of any one Anachropunk. All the same, it's a theme that crops up time and time again. To be part of any of the Anachropunks, some element of the real or imagined past has to be made "alternative" in some way to earn the punk moniker, or pull elements of the past forward in time to bring attention to them.

A Spoonful of Sugar

I shared a panel with Sarah Hans, writer and editor of the *Steampunk World* and *Steampunk Universe* anthologies. She pointed out that Steampunk tends to be more optimistic than its punk brethren. (Solarpunk was not part of the discussion, only the past-oriented punks.) That may make it harder for people to see the similarities. Don't forget, adding humor is a way to "punk" the status quo and it takes the sting out of reality. (See "Make it Funny") Jesters and stand-up comedians have a long history of telling hard truths through comedy. Never underestimate the power of laughter to open people to new ideas.

It's also important to go back to the source materials. Early science fiction problematized technology, but also dreamed big. With enough drive and resources, heroes and villains of the earlier adventures and scientific romances could accomplish anything. Many Steampunk writers look to that whimsy and optimism, and attempt to infuse their work with it. Real life is dark enough; it's okay to be drawn to the light sometimes.

Even so, this could be part of the reason there is a debate over whether Steampunk is in fact punk at all. The other Anachropunks tend toward the dystopian, so it can be hard to see where Steampunk can fit in when the focus can seem so different.

A Little Too Sweet?

Occasionally, I've seen criticism of Steampunk that it "glorifies" the Victorian era. The only thing I can think to say in response is, "Are you sure you've been reading Steampunk?"

We can all agree that Steampunk is more than just historical fiction (fiction written in the present about the past as it occurred). And not just because storytellers have the freedom to set their punk stories in a fantasy world that never existed. I believe in many cases, the people who make this criticism are in fact reading outside of the genre. For me at least, by definition, the *best* Steampunk that *truly* deserves that label *can't* glorify that past *without problematizing it at the same time* simply because it wouldn't be *punk*. (Note the added emphasis on "best.") That might be a little too circular to satisfy everybody, but it's my train of thought.

Even the Steampunk stories that involve the upper crust are constantly problematizing the time and place that inspired them. Women, minorities, differently-abled people, the poor, differing sexualities—they all get a voice in Steampunk in a way they never did with writers like Jules Verne and their scientific romances (fiction written in the past that speculated about the future). The books that have inspired the Steampunk genre are full of bias and ugly stereotypes. Writing a world without these stereotypes can function as a way of calling attention to them. Their absence in the story makes their presence in real life all the more pronounced. For instance, the Victorian era has a reputation for being a time of repressed sexual desire. If someone writes a story about someone of that era expressing unbridled passion, it breaks with the stereotype. As more of those stories are written, that becomes a less powerful act of rebellion. It isn't as shocking when you've seen it before.

I acknowledge it impossible to ignore the very visual nature of Steampunk, and for many, that is the sum total of their interest in this fandom. It began life as a literary genre, but it is an aesthetic that has captured the minds of makers and the attention of artists. In many ways, applying the aesthetic to just about anything does itself conjure this better, more tolerant world of Steampunk literary works. And let's not forget that Steampunk is a *fandom* and a *hobby*. People participate because it is *fun,* because it stimulates something in them. I also know that however people found their way to Steampunk, they rarely remain on the surface for long. The lectures at conventions that are the best attended are often the ones that look at the darker side of the era, and raise awareness about how bad the era was for the majority of people. Plus, there's nothing quite so punk as creating something and not letting anyone tell you not to. The writers and makers are putting their personal stamp on the fandom. (For a more in-depth discussion of this topic, see the final chapter in this book, Make it Yours.)

Okay, so back to those upper-crusters. This isn't to say that people in Steampunk works can't have a spiffing good time enjoying some of the finer things just because they are fine. Some people did live lives of luxury. And let's face it, they would have far more free time and resources to go on adventures than your average working class stiff. The same way it is easier to kill off the parent(s) of a protagonist than to deal with fully-formed relationships in the course of your story, making the main character a member of the upper echelons takes down many of the barriers real people would have faced.

However, as long as anything in those pages calls attention to some sort of social or historical issue, then I believe it's accurate to call it Steampunk. Or at minimum, recognize it as something Steampunk fans will *enjoy*. If a work truly does gloss over all negative aspects of the steam era or setting informed by it *in addition* to ignoring the distinct aesthetic, Steampunk probably isn't the best word to describe it.

I won't say that someone "can't" use Steampunk to describe it, only that it may not be the best descriptor. I feel the same way about movies like *Sky Captain and the World of Tomorrow*. Many people put that on lists of Steampunk movies, where I specifically leave it off. Yes, there are airships and giant robots, both things you could find in a Steampunk story. However, *aesthetically* that film bears a much closer resemblance to the Diesel or Deco eras. As someone with a minor in art history, I am more likely to see these differences in aesthetic than someone else, and I am aware that my level of education and general interests influence my decisions. So, while I wouldn't tell someone to remove *Sky Captain* from their list, I have my own personal parameters that keeps it off mine. And best of all, this doesn't stop me or anyone else from *enjoying* the movie.

In addition, I'd argue that critics of Steampunk should spend as much time looking at the villains as they do the heroes. Robber barons, war-mongers, cold-hearted scientists, and pirates bent on world domination—Steampunk heroes battle them all. More often than not, if a nasty Vic-wardian tidbit is included, it is the villain who does it. Writers use them to give voice to, and so to problematize, issues of the past through the mouthpiece of the "bad guy."

In Conclusion

If we are going to discuss the "punk" part of the word, then we get into general matters of the definition of Steampunk. It's important to recognize that if the meaning of "punk" is open for interpretation, the meaning of Steampunk is going to remain in flux alongside it. Punk meant (and means) different things to people in different parts of the world. It's no surprise that Steampunk would be the same way.

The final chapter of this book expands on the process of defining the parameters for Steampunk.

Chapter 4

The next section of this book will be looking at the 30+ years since the word Steampunk first appeared in print. Before we get into the time since the word existed, however, I thought it would be a great opportunity to pay homage to those things that could be considered to fit within the Steampunk canon but came before the 1987 date. Even K.W. Jeter, who made up the word, openly admits that it was happening with or without him. On his website, he says:

"Here's the deal: I didn't invent steampunk. I did, however

bumble into coining the word 'steampunk.' There's a lot of creativity, written and otherwise, and just general fun that's going on in regard to Victorian-themed fantasy & science fiction, and if a word I created has become attached as the portmanteau handle to all that, then I'm flattered. But it would still be going on, with or without that label."

As discussed in previous chapters, trying to define the boundaries of Steampunk is difficult. There is one hard and fast line that I am personally willing to draw in the sand, but others may not agree. This question comes up with some frequency:

Is science fiction of the Victorian era "Steampunk?"

My personal and very brief answer to this question is a resounding "no." I'm willing to be convinced otherwise, but here's my logic.

"Scientific Romances" (as these stories were called by their contemporaries) penned by the likes of Jules Verne, H.G. Wells, etc. were decidedly forward-looking. They were written largely about a near future the authors thought (or hoped, or feared, depending on the story) might just turn out to be possible. Steampunk, on the other hand, is more or less backward-looking. We are at a point technologically and intellectually beyond the period on which this genre draws. Even if a story is set at some point in the future, if the tech is circa the Industrial Revolution, it's harkening to the past.

Furthermore, Steampunk works often use archetypes and tropes created during the steam era, but use them to offer commentary on either the past or the present. Therefore, I see them as fundamentally different enterprises from the "classics" that created the archetypes.

However, Steampunk works often draw directly from Victorian-era fiction, so I'd like to take some time to explore these works as fodder for the imagination, as well as some of the adaptations that followed their creation.

A Few Words on Adaptation

Some of the best-loved works from the steam era were adapted to stage productions even during the author's lifetime. For instance, *The Strange Case of Doctor Jekyll and Mr. Hyde* by Robert Louis Stevenson hit the stage only a year after the novella was first published. The writer attended the production, then promptly stormed out in a huff.

In the book, he'd been careful never to say precisely what it was that the good doctor believed was so "evil" about himself (which in turn manifested as Mr. Hyde). In the play, they'd decided to show this evil by making Mr. Hyde a consummate womanizer. Stevenson was appalled that his "evil" character could be minimized by giving him such a trivial vice.

While vagueness works just fine in print, it really wouldn't have worked at all on stage. If you'd asked the playwright, not being able to choose some visual cues as to the nature of said "evil" would have ruined the play. The truth of the matter is that many wonderful books simply do not translate to a visual medium without there being some sort of concession to both the medium itself and audience expectations. In other words, the books almost always get at least a little bit "punked."

When it comes to Jekyll and Hyde, the more adaptations that were created, the more they tended to deviate. In the original, the reader doesn't know the connection between the two men, and the story is told by a third party. In most visual adaptations, there's no narrator at all save Jekyll and Hyde themselves, who are most often played by the same actor. This is totally at odds with the original, and fundamentally changes the audience's experience. (Though you would have trouble finding someone nowadays who didn't already know about Stevenson's twist.) Between the pressures of the particular medium, as well as the pressure to do something new, the stories change with each new adaptation.

Early Adaptations (and Re-Adaptations)

Though it may seem paradoxical of me, this is why I put the slew of *adaptations* of the 19th century classics more firmly into the Steampunk canon than the original works. Note I say "more firmly," which is to say that they don't necessarily fit well at all, but by dint of being adaptations there is potential for change. Furthermore, some would be more comfortably placed into one of the other Anachropunks other than "Steam," so you may disagree with the examples I have provided. All the same, these are some of the first film adaptations of works penned during the steam era, and are worth noting as inspiration for those who were destined to wear the Steampunk moniker later.

***Alice in Wonderland* (1903, early 1920s, 1931, and 1951)**

The book was first published by Lewis Carroll in 1865, and found its way to theaters first as an 8-minute film in 1903. It sticks close to the story, but as a silent film, it lacks the charm and resonance of Carroll's incredible language.

The adaptation in 1931 gave literal "voice" to the story, but apparently, the amateur American actors had difficulty replicating British accents. The 1930s saw several different plays, puppet shows, and other types of adaptations as "Alice

Fever" swept the English-speaking world.

Two decades later, Disney Studios gave it their best shot, but this time in animation. This was their 13th animated feature length film. Originally, Disney began work on an animated feature adaptation back in the 1930s, but abandoned the project. The idea was revived in the 1940s and came to fruition in 1951. This film is noted as one of the best ever made by that studio, and often hailed among the best adaptations of Alice in Wonderland ever made.

You're probably familiar with the film, but what most people don't know is that Walt Disney had already made a series of shorts in the early 1920s that paid homage to the story called "Alice Comedies."

Around the World in 80 Days (1919 and 1956)

It surprised me that this Jules Verne story was one of the first to be adapted to film. I'd assumed that so many different locations would have made filming it very expensive and time-consuming. The original story was written in 1873, and the first adaptation came out of Germany in 1919. Despite the World Wars, Germany was a major force in filmmaking during the first half of the 20th century. This version is a parody of the original story and originally had to go by the name "A Journey Around the World" due to a copyright kerfuffle with the Verne estate.

But the version you've probably seen came from Disney in 1956. Though this adaptation wasn't playing for laughs, the screenwriters did take liberties. The most obvious is the addition of a stop in Spain and Phileas Fogg's arrival by hot air balloon. Though this scene didn't appear in the original text, it may have been a nod to another Verne classic, *Five Weeks in a Balloon* (1863). To make space, they dropped a (rather lengthy) section of the story about the history of the Mormons. It would have been a long stretch of Passepartout sitting and listening, so I don't think any viewers minded!

The Mysterious Island (1929, 1941, and 1951)

The first film to tackle this Jules Verne tale in 1929 had the name, but bore little resemblance to the book. In many ways, it was more like a prequel to *20,000 Leagues Under the Sea*, except that [spoiler] the captain (here called "Dakkar" rather than Nemo) does die at the end of the story as he does in the book. This rendition was thought to be lost until a copy was discovered and preserved in Prague in 2013.

The 1941 film was made in Russia and follows the original text much more closely. A decade later, Columbia Pictures produced the first English language adaptation, but couldn't resist a little "punking" along the way. In addition to the pirates and natural phenomenon that threaten the shipwrecked heroes, aliens from Mercury also inhabit the island. They could fit in this extra plot because it ran as a serial and totaled over 250 minutes of run-time.

Treasure Island (1934 and 1950)

This is another of Stevenson's works has been popular on the silver screen. What it lacks in steam power, it makes up for through the "shipwrecked" trope. Several writers during the steam era penned tales of the poor, lost souls who came aground on a mysterious land. Personally, I'd love to see Steampunk embrace this more, but the authors seem to have felt more at home in urban settings.

CHAPTER 4

20,000 Leagues Under the Sea (1954)

This has to be one of, if not the most popular film adaptations of Jules Verne's work. Yet, it deviates sharply from the original in terms of the technology involved. Rather than relying on a chemical reaction to create electricity, Nemo's Nautilus is powered by a nuclear reactor. This choice likely reflected the enthusiasm at that time for a new technology rather than any issue with Verne's science. The film also makes the encounter with the giant squid into a much bigger event than in the text.

The Fabulous World of Jules Verne (1958)

This Czech film is a mish-mash of Verne's stories, but draws most heavily from the lesser known *Facing the Flag*.

Journey to the Center of the Earth (1959)

In the 1864 book by Jules Verne, an eccentric uncle and nephew team follow centuries-old directions to a tunnel that leads into the earth. This adaptation adds murder and conspiracy to what is more or less a travelogue. Competing factions are trying to prove the truth behind the claims and are willing to kill for it.

Earliest Novels Retroactively Called "Steampunk"

Ronald C. Clark spent much of his writing career focused on non-fiction. His favorite subjects included mountain climbing and biographies of historical figures, such as Charles Darwin and Sigmund Freud. However, in 1967, he published a book that many consider the first Steampunk novel. *Queen Victoria's Bomb* is an alternate history where the British develop the atom bomb during the Crimean War.

A few years later, Michael Moorcock gave the world the first installment in his "Nomads of the Time Stream" series. Time travel, like that found in the work of H. G. Wells, is the major focus of the series. However, there are other Steampunk staples as well, such as airships. In the first book, *Warlords of the Air*, we meet an Edwardian era soldier stationed in India. He travels to a parallel universe where World War I never happened. The second book, *The Land Leviathan*, originally carried the subtitle "A New Scientific Romance" as an homage to his predecessors. This book deals even more overtly with Britain's imperialist history.

In between Moorcock's second and third installments (*The Steel Tsar,* 1981), K. W. Jeter published his sequel to *The Time Machine* called *Morlock Night* in 1979. As Jeter and his compatriots straddle the time before and after the word Steampunk came into existence, I placed the discussion of their books in the next chapter. However, it is interesting to note that time travel itself appears to be an important gateway to these explorations of the Industrial era and the history altering implications of actions taken during that period. For an in-depth discussion of how to deal with altering history, see the "Make it Alternative" chapter later in this book.

How the West was Weirded

The same way Gaslamp fantasy could be considered a permutation of Steampunk, "Weird West" is also a genre that is intertwined with both. For many members of the baby boomer generation, and even before, their childhoods were full of romantic visions of the pioneer days acted out by the likes of John Wayne, Clint Eastwood, and Sam Elliott.

These silver screen dramas lost favor by the 1970s, but on the television, writers were already starting to play around with the format in 1964 in the form of *Wild, Wild West*. Though it has a cowboy-laden setting, the name is a pun based on the main character, James West. With the help of his partner and their gadget-filled train car, they spy on behalf of Ulysses S. Grant. This show blended the genres of Western and spy-thrillers such as James Bond, which were popular at the time. The show lasted for four seasons between 1964-1969. In addition, 1980 saw the making of TV-movies, *Wild Wild West Revisited* and *More Wild Wild West Revisited*.

The decline of the cowboy drama paired with its place in recent memory also paved the way for Mel Brooks' incredibly successful film, *Blazing Saddles*, released in 1974. This was a significant moment in film history, not just for the commentary on racial intolerance buried under the fart jokes, but also because it was the first time anyone "punked" the stalwart cowboy mythos in a movie. (On a side note, Brooks also released *Young Frankenstein* later that same year, which is of course a parody on Mary Shelley's foundational gothic scientific romance, *The Modern Prometheus* (AKA Frankenstein)).

Weird West is a genre unto itself, so I won't even attempt to go too far down that rabbit hole. However, it is worth mentioning it as both a cousin of Steampunk, as well as these two examples in particular because of their use of humor and action. Much of Weird West crosses over with horror, but both *Wild, Wild West* and *Blazing Saddles* have a much lighter tone that is more in line with much of the Steampunk genre as we know it today. For a deeper discussion of employing humor in

Steampunk, see the "Make it Funny" chapter later in this book.

Chapter 5

The First Decade 1987-1996

For this chapter, we'll be focusing on the mid-1980s through 1996, and especially on the literature that serves as the foundation for a genre that has since branched into fashion, music, and more. The quote below came from an editorial Jeter sent in to Locus Magazine in 1987. As I said previously, "Cyberpunk" that was very popular at the time, and Steampunk took its name from there.

> **PERSONALLY,** I think that Victorian fantasies are going to be the next **BIG THING** as long as we can come up with some collective term for **POWERS, BLAYLOCK,** and **MYSELF.** Something based on the appropriate **TECHNOLOGY** of the time; like **"STEAM-PUNKS"** *perhaps.*
> —K.W. JETER

(The image was part of the 30 Years of Steampunk exhibit created by Phoebe Darqueling and P.R. Chase.)

When I saw Jeter speak at the 2017 International Steampunk Symposium, he shared that it came as a complete surprise when others started using the word in the following years. It was actually his wife who first noticed and brought it to his attention. He'd more or less forgotten about it by that time.

Who are Powers, Blaylock, and Jeter?

Despite the Victorian London setting so often associated with Steampunk, these three "pillars" of the literary canon are all Americans. Perhaps this is why they could so readily and masterfully "punk" the steam era; they felt less loyalty to the history they were playing with. The story goes that the three of them would get together to bounce around ideas while attending California State University in the 1970s. All three of them shared an important resource that helped shape their Steampunk books, *London Labour and the London Poor* by Henry Mayhew.

Though *Infernal Devices* (1987) is most often pointed to as Jeter's seminal Steampunk work, he also wrote a "sequel" to H.G. Wells' *The Time Machine* called *Morlock Night* that was published in 1979. If you're not familiar, the "morlocks" are the segment of humanity that live underground, turning them into brutish beasts, and they work on behalf of the Eloi, who became childlike over the centuries of not fending for themselves. The time traveler in Wells' work encounters them far into the future. I loved that Jeter's book asks the question "What if the Morlocks used the time machine themselves?" He paints them as every bit as smart as the Eloi, but far more dangerous than Wells ever did.

Anubis Gates by Tim Powers followed in 1983. This book has not only time travel, but a healthy dose of Egyptian mysticism that was incredibly popular during the steam era. It begins in the 1980s, but quickly turns into a man's quest to return to his own time to escape the (quite authentic) squalor and exploitation of urban life.

Homunculus came out in 1986 and was written by James Blaylock. "Homunculus" is a term from Alchemy that refers to a little person created from scratch by an alchemist. In this case, however, it refers to a tiny alien. This is actually the second book in Blaylock's loosely related Steampunk trilogy that includes *The Digging Leviathan* (1984) and *Lord Kelvin's Machine* (1992), though the first book garnered less attention than books 2-3 in the series.

As you can see, even early on there was a huge variety of subjects and styles within Steampunk as it gained traction with publishers and readers in the 1980s.

The Difference Engine, AKA "Cyberpunk set in the Past"

Even though many would place this 1990 release by William Gibson and Bruce Sterling squarely in the Steampunk camp, when they wrote it, they had another idea. The story focuses on computer technology, the basic mechanics of which were created during the steam era. In their tale, the Internet and highly sophisticated surveillance systems already exist.

They use this premise to explore what "Big Brother" would have looked like in the past. For this reason, it is rooted in Cyberpunk, which takes a largely dystopian and grim view when it comes to the influence of computers on society. On the other hand, it takes place in Victorian-era London and uses references to historical figures to situate it in the same way many Steampunk books do. It is one of those books that is clearly Anachropunk, but it can be hard to pinpoint exactly where it belongs.

1995 Was a Great Year for Steampunk Books

All of a sudden, several books hit the scene at the same time. *The Golden Compass* (AKA *Northern Lights* to British readers) was the first book ever to be described outright as Steampunk as it was being marketed. This indicates that the term had become popular enough by this time to mean something to the reading public.

This first installment in Philip Pullman's "His Dark Materials" series takes place in a parallel universe, but later in the series you meet people from our own world as well. The books center on a truth-telling device and the religious authorities who will stop at nothing to keep the truth away from the general public.

The Steampunk Trilogy by Paul Di Filippo came out soon after. It consists of a trio of novellas called "Victoria," "Hottentots," and "Walt & Emily." Reviewer Antonia Urias put it this way:

"[The Steampunk Trilogy] contains three bizarre and occasionally humorous novels taking the reader from Queen Victoria's amphibian doppelganger to racist naturalists and black magic, and finally the interdimensional love story of Emily Dickinson and Walt Whitman."

The third foundational 1995 release was called *The Diamond Age*. It carries the subtitle "A Young Lady's Illustrated Primer", which references a book that is central to the story. In this tale, a father risks his life to get the book for his daughter even though it is reserved only for the elites. He soon finds himself embroiled in a conspiracy and he has no choice but to keep going down the rabbit hole if he is to protect her from the consequences of his actions.

Though the novel *The Prestige* is rarely mentioned in lists from this time, it is worth noting that it also came out this year. For more information on that story, see the next chapter where I discuss the 2006 film adaptation.

Steampunk in Other Media

It didn't take long before Steampunk started to permeate visual and interactive media as well as literature.

The early 90's saw the birth of an amazingly imaginative TV series that, like so many other of Fox's creations, was canceled far too soon. "The Adventures of Brisco County, Jr." aired between 1993-1994. It may be most accurately described as Weird West, but as we we've already seen, the two genres are intertwined.

"Brisco County," as the program is often called, shares several traits with the series and films in the *Wild, Wild West* franchise from the 1960s and 70s. A man gives up lawyering to become a smart-talking, anachronistic bounty hunter in the American West circa 1893. Several of the episodes feature a futuristic device called The Orb, and this tech, plus the emphasis on humor thanks to the fabulous Bruce Campbell, help to secure its place in the Steampunk canon.

On the big screen, we have to look to France to find Steampunk at this time. In 1996, the surreal nightmare *La Cité des Enfants Perdus* (The City of Lost Children) came out. It centers on a "mad scientist" who is unable to sleep, so he steals the dreams of children. It doesn't have much in the way of steam tech per se, but the scientific mind run amok is a tried and true trope taken straight from the 19th century.

For people looking for something a little more interactive, they didn't have to look any farther than *Space 1889*. This tabletop game has a suite of miniatures that players can use to stage combat on Mars. It was first released in the early 90s, but since then there have been several sequels and expansions to the original game.

In 1993, a Swedish pen-and-paper role-playing game called *Mutant Chronicles* made its way to America. Like *Space 1889*, it also features space travel, but takes place in the distant future. A mysterious force called "the Dark Symmetry" keeps computers or any other intelligent machines from functioning, leaving the inhabitants of the solar system to survive using older tech. A movie by the same name came out in 2008 but wasn't received very well by critics or movie-goers. The gaming community appears to still enjoy it, however. Licensing for the game has bounced around to different companies over the years, and the third rendition was released in 2017.

Chapter 6

The Second Decade 1997-2006

Now, we embark on the decade spanning the mid-1990s to the mid-2000s in which Steampunk continued to branch out from literature and found a home in fashion and graphic novels. Plus, we see the birth of the first online forums for connecting Steampunk fans.

Steampunk Fashion

Steampunk jumped from the pages of books into the realm of wearable art sometime in the mid- to late-1990s. Fashion student Kit Stolen is one well-known example. He wore distressed Victorian style clothes paired with his own unique hair creations (called "falls") and caused quite a sensation in the New York club scene. Large-scale events wouldn't show up in earnest for a few years yet, but daring creators like Stolen paved the way for the rest of us to enjoy our corsets and top hats later on.

Visual Media

During this time, we see Steampunk making an even bigger leap from words to visual representations. Graphic novels show up for the first time, as well as some film and TV. I found it more straightforward to group them by year rather than the type of media because some of them crossed over from one to the other within this decade.

The League of Extraordinary Gentlemen

In 1999, writer Alan Moore (*The Watchmen*) and illustrator Kevin O'Neill paired up to create the first LoEG graphic novels. The story is set in 1898 in the aftermath of the events of Dracula. Mina Harker is recruited by Campion Bond (a predecessor of James Bond) to lead a unique group of "extraordinary" literary figures. She recruits the likes of Allan Quartermain, Dr. Jekyll/Mr. Hyde, The Invisible Man, and Captain Nemo to join her to fight Fu Manchu in the first collection. Volume II centers on the events of *War of the Worlds*. This two-volume collection of comics is brimming with literary characters and settings from the 19th century. And much in the same vein as the first Steampunk books, this series definitely has a dark side.

The 2003 film by the same name, however, was pitched as more of a family affair. Sean Connery plays Quartermain and as the one with the star power, he ended up totally usurping Mina as the leader of the group. They also added a big role for Tom Sawyer as a CIA agent. Many fans of comics hated the movie because it shed all of its darkness, and film critics didn't love it either. Still, it's a fun homage to the literature of the steam era and often visually stunning.

Wild, Wild West Movie (1999)

This is another movie that checks several Steampunk boxes, but ran into problems with fans. This reimagining of the 1960s Western-spy crossover as an adventure comedy rubbed many the wrong way. The franchise centers on James West, a sheriff who works for Ulysses S. Grant. At the time, Will Smith, who played West, was one of the hottest actors in Hollywood, and Kevin Kline was on a similar hot streak when he played West's sidekick. It culminates in a mad scientist on a rampage in his giant mechanical spider. I personally loved this movie when I first saw it. Then again, I'd never seen the original series, so I wasn't suffering from any dashed expectations. The movie is definitely a comedy. I can see why someone looking for James Bond in the Wild West could be disappointed. (But still, *giant mechanical spider* = awesome. Am I right?)

Sleepy Hollow (1999)

The story of "Sleepy Hollow" first appeared in print in 1820 as a short story. Since then, it's gone on to be one of the most enduring American ghost stories of all time. In Washington Irving's original tale, a hapless schoolteacher in New York state is pursued by a ghost in 1790. In the film, the character of Ichabod Crane has been fundamentally altered. (Except for the hapless part.) He's a police constable in 1799 in New York City. Unlike his comrades, he's convinced science and reason lay at the heart of solving crimes.

To test his claims, his superiors send him to a small town where a rash of mysterious murders has broken out. He packs his chemistry set and goofy-looking spectacles, and heads to the beleaguered hamlet of Sleepy Hollow. He meets with the town elders, who assure Crane the murderer is not only a ghost, but one that takes the heads of his victims with him as a souvenir. And in true Tim Burton fashion, the Horseman (Christopher Walken) is depicted as the thing all the other nightmares would be scared of.

Girl Genius (2001-Present)

The husband and wife team of Phil and Kaja Foglio created this series in 2001. It may be more accurately described as Gaslamp Fantasy, a term that Kaja Foglio created to describe the series as it straddles the line between sci-fi and fantasy. It's about Agatha Clay, a harried science student in a semi-Victorian setting and carries the tagline "Adventure, Romance, MAD SCIENCE!" It started off as a black and white print book, added color in issue 3, and jumped to the web in 2005. You can read the entire series from the beginning, and it is still updated every week.

Dark Portals: The Chronicles of Vidoqc (2001)

In the original French, this film is called simply *Vidoqc* because this name is famous in their history. Eugene Francois Vidoqc was a real police investigator in the first half of the

19th century and is largely recognized as the "father of forensic science." His methods were so advanced, in fact, that people thought he dabbled in the occult. This association is the inspiration behind the film, which is both gritty and beautiful. The structure is unusual and non-linear, and it is among my favorite films of all time.

The Amazing Screw-on Head (2002)

Dark Horse comics later released this dark comedy by Mike Mignola (*Hellboy*) about a secret agent working in Abraham Lincoln's service in 2002. True to his name, Screw-on Head has a removable head that can be installed in a number of bodies with different capabilities. A few years later, the SyFy channel released the pilot for an animated series. Unfortunately, despite the voice talent of Paul Giamatti, David Hyde Pierce, and Patton Oswalt, it never made it past the first episode.

Firefly (2002) and *Serenity* (2005)

This Fox television series and the fan-driven film that followed has to be the top of the "is it or isn't it Steampunk?" list. With its far-future setting, incredible speed of travel, and occasional über high-tech plot points, I can see why some may say no. On the other hand, there's also a train heist, cattle rustling, gun slinging, and bank robbing, so it has an undeniable Western feel to it.

The basic premise is that the human race left behind our own solar system a long time ago and has settled in a new one. There are the core planets, which have everything you'd expect in a futuristic, computer-driven setting. However, there are also the border planets that are only recently terra-formed and made fit for human habitation. Out on the brink, life mirrors the frontier days in Earth-that-was. The show follows a crew of misfits as they try to stay out from under the thumb of the core and make a living, which may or may not be honest.

Steamboy (2004)

The director, Katsuhiro Otomo, is best known for his cyberpunk directorial debut *Akira* in 1988. I have a great respect for graphic artists and animators, and the creators of this film lend all of the attention to detail and breath-taking beauty to the Victorian era you could hope for. The settings are primarily the Crystal Palace of the Great Exhibition in London and inside an enormous "steam castle," and they have been rendered with incredible detail.

Otomo takes a few liberties with those pesky historical facts, but you can't go letting the facts get in the way of a good story. For instance, Steamboy takes place in 1866, but the Great Exhibition took place in 1851. Likewise you get to see Tower Bridge totally destroyed, but it was not built until 1894. I recommend you just chalk it up to being an alternative Victorian era and enjoy the ride.

Van Helsing (2004)

Gabriel Van Helsing (Hugh Jackman) is a monster hunter with a mysterious past. He is employed by the Catholic church to seek out and destroy evil, but remembers nothing before he was charged with his holy quest. As far as I can tell, the only thing this Van Helsing has in common with the Dutch doctor and do-gooder Abraham Van Helsing of Bram Stoker's novel *Dracula* is the name.

The film starts with an homage to classic black and white movies as an angry mob attacks castle Frankenstein in 1887.

Sommers' twist is that the good doctor's financial backer is none other than Count Dracula. Van Helsing enters the movie with an epic confrontation with a truly monstrous Mr. Hyde on the rooftop of Notre Dame. Later, Van Helsing is charged with slaying Dracula in time to protect the souls of the Valerius family, who vowed they would never rest until the vampire met his demise.

Brothers Grimm (2005)

I am a big fan of Terry Gilliam (who wrote and directed *Monty Python and the Holy Grail*, among other things) and he definitely does not disappoint in this, his first PG-13 movie. He actually rewrote much of the *Brothers Grimm* screenplay, but did not receive credit. Though the story is more magical than sci-fi, I think it deserves a nod as a Steampunk film because the Grimm's stories were so important to the 19th century and the people's beliefs in supernatural forces. (See "Make it Supernatural")

The city of Karlstadt is in need of heroes to fight a witch that is terrorizing their town and the Grimm brothers arrive to save the day. Too bad for the townsfolk that the witch is a hoax and the brothers are scam artists. Jacob has spent his life collecting folk tales, but Wilhelm is an avid skeptic and is only out to make a living. Soon, the brothers are forcibly recruited by the French, who occupied Germany during the Napoleonic Wars (1803-1815). A general tells the brothers of a town called Marbaden and the nine children who have disappeared. According to the peasants, a supernatural force took their children, but the French believe it is another con artist like the Grimms. They have to catch the culprit or answer for their own crimes. Too bad for them some fairy tales do come true…

The Five Fists of Science (2006)

Dark Horse published another Steampunk graphic novel gem with Mark Twain and Nikola Tesla in the starring roles. This is a tight little book that doesn't waste any words, which means that all of the front-pages are more than just prologue. If you pick this one up (and I recommend you do), make sure you check out the short biographies of the real people involved, as well as the letter shared between Twain and Tesla that inspired this story full of giant robots and Lovecraftian beasties.

The Illusionist (2006)

Though this film came out in direct competition with *The Prestige* (see below), I've noticed it does not often appear on lists of Steampunk films. This oversight may be due to using Vienna as the setting, but I believe this film deserves a place in the Steampunk canon. The screenplay is loosely based on a short story by Pulitzer Prize winner Stephen Millhauser called "Eisenheim the Magician." The character of Eisenheim is accused of necromancy and truly harnessing the powers of the supernatural because he won't reveal how he does his tricks. Many of the illusions described in the story and shown in the film were real tricks done by magicians of the era, such as Jean Eugene Robert-Houdin. (Harry Houdini took his stage name from this foundational magician.)

The antagonist of the film is a fictional prince of the Austria-Hungarian empire, Leopold, so there's a little bit of punking history for you. This character is based on the real prince Rudolf who died in 1889, ten years before the film is set. Like the character of Leopold, Rudolf had a mistress who died under shadowy circumstances and the mystery was never solved. The injection of a love story, which is the true focus of the film, was not part of the original short story. So, it is another example of adaptation "punking" the original as it moved between mediums.

The Prestige (2006)

This film is based on a 1995 novel by the same name and written by Christopher Priest. It's about two rival magicians in the late 1890s. (The original story behind *The Illusionist* also featured rival magicians, but they obviously backed away from that concept in the film.) The two seek to outdo each other in a series of escalating illusions, culminating in one called "The Transported Man." The quest for the key behind the trick leads one of the men to the doorstep of Nikola Tesla, who reveals a new invention. I won't say any more than that in case I ruin the surprises in store for the audience.

When the inevitable comparisons between *The Illusionist* and *The Prestige* happened upon their release, fans largely favored the latter. Though it makes some sense to compare them because of the timing of the releases and the time periods, they seek to fill completely different niches. *The Illusionist* is a love story about a man who tantalizes a world on the brink of modernity with the suggestion of the supernatural. *The Prestige* is a psychological thriller mashed up with science fiction. The only thing they really have in common is magicians as central characters, but both have a lot to offer in terms of inspiration for Steampunk fans in the ways they handled the intersection of history and fiction.

CHAPTER 6

Steampunk Hits the Web

In 2006, the first dedicated Steampunk forum was established. Though the creator no longer plays an active role or updates it regularly, you can still visit "Brass Goggles." This was an important step in the evolution of Steampunk as a community rather than a string of independent people. People could swap tips about making props and costumes, recommend books, and plan get-togethers in a streamlined way.

And Then Came the Music

Steampunk music is incredibly hard to define. Like Steampunk itself, it is an eclectic mix of past, present, and future, and has the punk attitude that no one can tell them who or what they are. I think this quote by "Lord Baron Joseph C.R. Vourteque IV" from SteampunkChicago.com does a good job of explaining it:

"It is not so much a genre as a collective of musicians and artists who relate to each other under the same DIY, every-man ethos with an aesthetic that ranges somewhere between 1870 and 1930."

There were some groups with a "neo-Victorian" sound before the decade we're exploring in this chapter, but the early to mid- 2000s saw many groups form who are still performing today. Rather than trying to pin down or group these bands by style, I'm going to list them alphabetically and invite you to explore their music for yourself. For further discussion on music in Steampunk, see the "Make it Musical" chapter.

This is a list of the earliest Steampunk bands, but is by no means comprehensive.

Abney Park - Formed 1997, first Steampunk album 2008, still active

Beats Antique - Formed 2007, still active

Caravan Palace - First album 2008, still active

Diego's Umbrella - Formed 2001, still active

Doctor Steel - Active 1999-2011

Frenchy and the Punk (AKA The Gypsy Nomads) - Formed 2005, still active

H.U.M.A.N.W.I.N.E. - Formed 2002, still active

Insomniac Folklore - Formed 2001, still active

Jill Tracy - 1995, still active

The Men That Will Not Be Blamed For Nothing - Formed 2008, still active

Mr. B the Gentleman Rhymer - 2007, still active

Professor Elemental - 2005, still active

Rasputina - Formed 1992, still active

Steam Powered Giraffe - Formed 2008, still active

Sunday Driver - Formed 2000, still active

This Way to the Egress - Formed 2008, still active

Thomas Truax - 2000, still active

Unextraordinary Gentlemen - Formed 2007, still active

Vernian Process - Formed 2003, still active

Veronique Chevalier - 2005, still active

Voltaire (AKA Aurelio Voltaire Hernandez) - 1998, still active

CHAPTER 6

The Rise of Steampunk Events

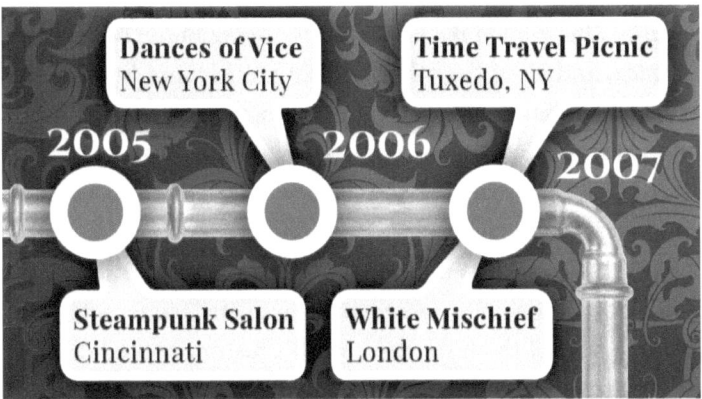

Steampunk's permeation of the music scene went hand in hand with the demand for entertainment at Steampunk-themed events. Fans weren't satisfied with simply reading about airships and clever (if impossible) gadgets, they wanted to live and breathe Steampunk "in the flesh." Some of these events were small-scale monthly gatherings, while others were huge conventions lasting all weekend. Nowadays, you can probably find some sort of Steampunk gathering in every one of the 50 states and in countries all over the world. It has grown from a solitary hobby to a whole community that loves to get together and have a great time.

What You Do at a Steampunk Convention?

In addition to enjoying the musical stylings of Steam-powered *Giraffe, This Way to the Egress, Victor & the Bully, Nightwatch Paradox*, and all of the other amazing musicians, Steampunk events lend themselves to a variety of other stage acts. There's often at least one magician or "mad scientist" doing a demonstration of arcane medical quackery. I've also seen plenty of circus acts and aerial performers wowing crowds at places like the International Steampunk Symposium and the Edwardian Ball. And especially in recent years, burlesque acts have become part of the festivities. With a history rooted directly in the "steam era," it comes as no surprise that this sort of performance has found a home.

Sound too noisy? No problem! You can always find a lecture to attend. I've been to a wide variety of talks ranging from the role of madness in the works of Edgar Allan Poe, to demos on pugilism and cane-fighting, to the bloody history of tea, to the ins and outs of alchemy. Steampunk covers a wide range of topics and areas of crossover, so no doubt you can find at least one presentation that will tickle your fancy.

Many events also have game rooms that feature tabletop games. These could be pen and paper RPGs, board games, and sometimes even live action role playing. TeslaCon is famous for its hugely interactive LARPing track in their annual event in Wisconsin, and they have even started to publish books in the world of the game.

If you're looking for some friendly and whimsical opportunities to compete, several sports have also emerged. Tea-dueling (and occasionally the spin-off, "coffee jousting") can be found at almost every large Steampunk event. To play, all you need is some tea and some biscuits. Competitors dunk their cookies, then play a game of "chicken" to see who can go longer without taking a bite. But watch out! If the cookie crumbles before you get it into your mouth, you lose.

The Maker and Steampunk are a Match Made in Heaven

Even though it began as a literary genre, many people find their way to Steampunk through the Maker Movement. The technology of Steampunk is largely mechanical and simple enough that even newbies can figure out how to make something go using gears. Pair this with the long tradition of beautiful, hand-crafted items from this time, and many makers are motivated to give it a whirl. Polished wood, inlaid brass, supple leather—they all have a place in Steampunk. Many of the competitions at conventions involve building something, then bringing it along to show off or pit against others.

My personal favorite is the races. I've seen people race both homemade dirigibles and "teapot racers" (remote control cars stripped of their bodies and replaced by tea pots) around obstacles courses. Weekend at the Asylum in the UK also invites people to race full-sized contraptions that are pedal-powered. Makers can also compete to see who has the coolest "mod" of a Nerf gun, and who crafted the best "vampire hunting kit."

And let's not forget the fabulous clothes! Though by no means a requirement, many people attend Steampunk events simply for the opportunity to wear and appreciate costumes. There are often competitions and fashion shows for people to show off their skills.

Chapter 7

The Third Decade 2007–Present

Now, we're going to take a look at the last 10-ish years and how this genre has exploded in popular culture. You'll notice I am no longer attempting to tell you about all of the books. That's because there are now literally thousands of them. Instead, I focus on a few that I see as having an important impact on the genre as a whole or were adapted for the screen. Though books are more numerous, films and television are both more accessible and can more easily carry and promote Steampunk as an aesthetic.

The Media Starts Noticing Steampunk

In the mid-2000s, news outlets first started to report on Steampunk as not only a genre, but an entire community and movement. Some folks who had been fans since the beginning were worried about how the exposure could "dilute" the fandom, while others welcomed the attention as a chance to bring more people into the fold. Either way, many members of the general public were first introduced to the word "Steampunk" thanks to these and other articles like them.

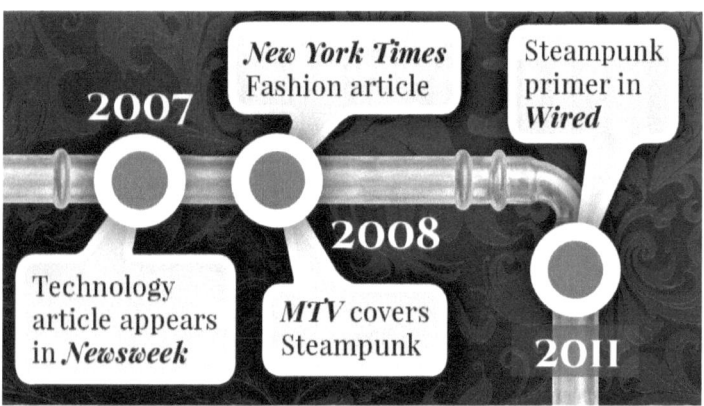

Steampunk Explodes in 2009

Many of the books that are now considered cornerstones of the Steampunk genre came out in 2009. For instance, Scott Westerfeld's *Leviathan* and accompanying sequels imagine an alternative World War I full of incredible machines that never existed pitted against the "Darwinists" who favor genetic manipulation.

CHAPTER 7

But one of the most noticeable things about 2009 for me was to see how many female writers were added to the list of Steampunk books. *Boneshaker* by Cherie Priest takes place in an alternate Seattle that has suffered from an outbreak of a strange gas that turns people into zombies. It follows a mother who is looking for her lost son and is every bit a horror series as it is Steampunk.

On the other end of the spectrum, we find Gail Carriger's *Soulless*. In this book about a world where vampires and werewolves are not only out in the open, but part of British politics, there are a lot more laughs than screams. The main character, Alexia Tarrabotti, is a delightful "spinster" who has the uncanny ability to nullify the magical aspects of others, and her exploits continue with several more books in The Parasol Protectorate series. In this series, as well as Carriger's YA series called Finishing School, clever women employ their wits and a suite of gadgets to battle evil, and happen to occasionally find love along the way.

"The Parasol Protectorate" has since made a jump from novels to graphic novels, and there are a few other long-running series worth noting that made their debut during or around 2009. *Grandville* by Bryan Talbot is a Hugo Award-winning graphic novel series that features anthropomorphic animals solving crimes during an alternative Napoleonic War. The final installment was released in 2017.

The Boston Metaphysical Society began as a web comic in 2013, and then to independent printing. In 2018, the graphic novels were picked up by a publisher, and author Madeleine Holly-Rosing also recently put out her first novel set in that world. As I'm sure you gleaned from the title, it involves a supernaturally-imbued Boston as the setting circa 1895.

Husband and wife team Tom and Nimue Brown brought the creepy, fictional world of the island *Hopeless, Maine* to life in graphic novel form around the same time. Their stories are rather surreal, with lovely and often macabre illustrations to match. They have also since branched out into other media, including a game. This kind of bouncing from media to media is becoming increasingly common nowadays in and out of Steampunk, and it allows fans to interact with their favorite characters and stories in a variety of ways.

Soon after, we see the first non-fiction books dedicated to Steampunk. In 2010, *Steampunk Emporium* was released. It had a focus on handicrafts and helping people give their creations a distinctive Steampunk style. And most diehard Steampunk fans own a copy of *The Steampunk Bible*, which came out in 2011. This collection of essays offers a wide view of the aesthetic and genre, and helped to inform the 30 Years of Steampunk exhibit and the series of articles this chapter is based on.

With the advent of the digital age, podcasting and vlogging (video blogging) also became platforms for discussing Steampunk. There are entire channels devoted to nothing but Steampunk, as well as bookcasters dabbling in Steampunk for their reviews. I already mentioned the rise of indie film-making, and this also includes documentaries about Steampunk showing up on major networks, like PBS, as well as popping up around the web to delight and inform potential fans.

CHAPTER 7

Steampunk in TV Series

Steampunk didn't just creep, but exploded onto the small screen during its third decade.

The Murdoch Mysteries (2008-?)
CityTV (Canada)
This drama is set in Toronto, Canada in the 1890s and 1990s. It's based on a series of novels by Maureen Jennings that began in 1997. The titular character is a methodical and logical detective with a penchant for creating gadgets that are slightly ahead of their time. He solves crimes with the help of a female coroner and some delightfully quirky coppers. Though it is a drama, there is a subtle sense of humor woven into episodes.

Warehouse 13 (2009-2014)
SyFy Network
This show also started airing in the pivotal year of 2009. Though it takes place in the present, the objects that are kept in the warehouse often have an origin in the real or imagined history of the 19th century. The electric gun wielded by the agents and the fantastical computer system at the heart of their missions are both undeniably Steampunk. Plus, a gender-swapped H.G. Wells who was frozen in time is an important character. Though the series is by no means exclusively Steampunk, it clearly borrows from the aesthetic and the time period from which more overtly Steampunk works draw.

Dracula (2013-2014)
NBC
This re-imagining of Bram Stoker's character has him posing

as an American entrepreneur who wants to bring modern science to Victorian society. He's especially interested in the new technology of electricity. Which makes sense when you think about how he's confined to darkness. His other reason for coming to London is to take revenge on those who cursed him with immortality centuries earlier. He meets Mina and becomes infatuated with her. Between this distraction and the machinations of a vampire hunter, his plans may come crashing down around him. I have heard some hemming and hawing about the costumes in NBC's Dracula because they aren't "period" enough. Personally, I think that is part of what makes it steampunk rather than a period drama and therefore way more interesting. The sets and clothes are absolutely gorgeous.

Penny Dreadful (2014-2016)
Showtime

If you are a lover of the macabre side of the steam era, you will absolutely adore Penny Dreadful. It's a bit like taking most of the superstitions of the Vic-wardian era and throwing them into a blender. Which sounds like it could be a terrible idea, but the execution is very compelling. Characters include literary characters such as Victor Frankenstein and his creature, Dorian Gray, and Dr. Jekyll.

The Frankenstein Chronicles (2015-2017)
ITV Encore (Britain)

Though this show has Frankenstein in the title, it isn't a retelling of Mary Shelley's classic gothic tale. Instead, it centers on a river policeman several decades after the book takes place, and Shelley herself is a character in the first season. The police are investigating a string of strange crimes and stitched together bodies that appear to be the work of someone trying to unlock life after death and inspired by the story of Doctor Frankenstein. The show focuses on the darker side of the era, but unlike Penny Dreadful, the issues are rooted in the social inequality and squalor of the past rather than superstitions.

The Alienist (2018)
TNT

This show is based on a 1994 book by Caleb Carr and of the same title. The story takes place in New York City circa 1896 and features appearances by historical figures such as J.P. Morgan and a young Theodore Roosevelt. The main character is an alienist, a precursor to a criminal profiler in the steam era. He uses early forensic methods and pointed interviewing methods to investigate. With the help of New York's first female police officer (Dakota Fanning) and a newspaper illustrator (Luke Evans), they work together to solve the mystery of disappearing street children.

Carnival Row (2019-?)
Amazon Original

In place that isn't quite England in a time that isn't quite Victorian, tensions over fae immigrants are running high. After Tirnanog was discovered several decades prior, humans waged a war over that land and the supernatural creatures who called it home. Now, the refugees like Vignette Stonemoss, a librarian turned to criminal, are trying to make new lives for themselves in the human world. A Jack-the-Ripper type killing spree but where the victims are fae, a police constable works against his department's hostility to the fae in order to investigate. But he finds far more than just prejudices lurking in the foggy streets of Carnival Row.

Doctor Who

Plus, there are several episodes of the much-loved *Dr. Who* that are definitely intended to be Steampunk. Here are a few worth watching.

The Unquiet Dead (Episode 159, 9th Doctor)

The Doctor and Rose Tyler team up with Charles Dickens to solve a ghost story in 1869.

"Tooth and Claw" (Episode 169, 10th Doctor)

In 1879, The Doctor lands in Scotland and Queen Victoria is in danger from a werewolf attack.

"The New Doctor" (Episode 199 (Christmas Special), 10th Doctor)

The Doctor meets, well, The Doctor, or at least someone who claims to be, at Christmastime in 1851. The cybermen are at it again, and together the Doctors must save Christmas.

"Vincent and the Doctor" (Episode 210, 11th Doctor)

The Doctor takes Amy Pond to visit a Vincent Van Gogh exhibit, and they spy something in a painting that doesn't belong there. So, they head to 1890 to find out the origin of the terrible face in the window.

"Christmas Carol" (Episode 213 (Christmas Special) 11th Doctor)

The Doctor must take a page out of Dickens' book and soften

the soul of a miser to save Amy and Rory.

"The Doctor's Wife" (Episode 216, 11th Doctor)

Ok, this one isn't exactly Steampunk but it is my favorite episode and the old-meets-new vibe plus the junkyard in which it takes place appeals to my Steampunk side. Plus, it was written by my all-time favorite author, Neil Gaiman.

"A Town Called Mercy" (Episode 228, 11th Doctor)

This space-western fusion episode features a cyborg and the Doctor as sheriff of a small town.

"The Snowmen" (Episode 231, 11th Doctor)

It's just snow, right? Wrong! In 1892 the snow comes to life and sinister snowmen are on the loose.

"On Thin Ice" (Episode 264, 12the Doctor)

The Doctor takes his student to a frost fair in 1814, but there's something hungry hiding beneath the frozen surface of the Thames.

Recurring Characters: The Paternoster Gang

In "A Good Man Goes to War" (Episode 218), the Doctor calls upon compatriots from across time and space to aid him in rescuing Amy Pond from Demon's Run. Among them are Vastra, a Silurian (reptilian predecessors to the human race asleep in the center of the Earth), her maid/lover/badass Jenny Flint and a Sontaran (who I refer to as "the Mr. Potato heads of space") named Commander Strax. In Victorian times, they join forces and fight crime, sometimes alongside the Doctor.

Steampunk at the Cinema

Though some would not consider the following movies to be Steampunk in the strictest sense, I decided to include them because there are things there that Steampunk and Gaslamp Fantasy fans will enjoy. One exciting aspect of this decade of Steampunk in movies is that we see not only steam era works being reimagined, but Steampunk books themselves finding their way to the screen.

Although this section focuses primarily on Hollywood films, it's also important to mention the growing number of independent short and full-length films out there that employ a Steampunk theme or aesthetic. YouTube and Vimeo have tons of different options if you want a little Steampunk snippet, be it live action or animated. Creating digital works from scratch, as well as film editing software being both more sophisticated and affordable, many Steampunk creators are finding filmmaking as an outlet and method for adding their voice to the scene. Some of these films have been featured at major festivals and won awards.

The Golden Compass (2007)

I shared a little about this story in an earlier chapter, but in case you skipped it, the premise deals with parallel universes. The characters exist in a world that is both like and totally different from our own. Though our worlds exist side by side, the technology and some of the customs have a decidedly steam era feel to them. The main character, Lyra, grows up on the grounds of Jordan College at Oxford (which doesn't exist) and travels to the far North to defeat a diabolical group of child-snatchers.

Unfortunately for fans, the next two installments were never made. As the series progresses, it delves into questions of metaphysics and puts the religious institutions of Lyra's world into the role of villain. Our own Catholic church opposed the films, and whether their pressure or a less-than-stellar box office performance killed the franchise, we'll never know.

However, a television series called His Dark Materials began airing in 2019. This is a good example of how adapting to the screen can change things. There are two main characters in the series, but in the books they are completely separate for a lot of the time. In the show, they began weaving in Lyra's counterpart from the beginning, and I think this was a great choice. The show also does not shy away from the heartbreaking plot points that the movie left out.

9 (2009)

In 2005, filmmaker Shane Acker released a short film called "9" that was nominated for an Academy Award. Four years later, Focus Features released a feature-length version that was nominated for an Annie Award for best animated effects. In a post-apocalyptic wasteland, the scientist who accidentally brought about the end of humanity uses alchemy to create nine dolls. He gives them each a portion of his soul to bring them to life, and when the last one wakes, the story begins. Though it is animated, this is a dark film that earns its PG-13 rating.

Pride and Prejudice and Zombies (2009 book, 2016 movie)

Author Seth Grahame-Smith wrote two wonderful mashups where he added supernatural elements to something established in the steam era, this one and *Abraham Lincoln: Vampire Hunter*. However, he didn't come up with the idea himself.

Quirk Books editor Jason Rekulak saw the potential for taking public domain books and giving them a makeover with horror elements. He handed the project off to Grahame-Smith and when bloggers got wind of the project, people got very excited, paving the way for the film a few years later. Grahame-Smith uses the original story as a framework and even credits Jane Austen as his co-author, but adds in suspense and gore to put a new spin on the story.

The Adventures of Adele Blanc-Sec (2010)

Adele Blanc-Sec is a comic book hero who was created in the 1970s by Jacque Tardi. She started out as a foil for a different female lead character, but Tardi decided he liked writing Adele better and made her the star instead. The most recent graphic novel was released in 2007, and a film directed by Luc Besson followed in 2010.

In the movie, we first meet Adele on an expedition to Egypt. Her male compatriots try to ditch her but she soon proves she is the most capable one there. She leads them deep into the mummy's tomb. Adele is not on a search for riches, she has her heart set on a certain mummy whom she hopes can be revived. She needs him to save the life of her catatonic sister. I know, it doesn't sound like the most practical of plans, but she knows a man who has been honing his psychic abilities for just such an occasion.

While Professor Espérandieu is flexing his psychic muscles back in Paris, he inadvertently connects to the dormant life inside a dinosaur egg. Suddenly, a baby pterodactyl is set loose into the skies above the City of Lights. The professor is accused of the "crimes" that result and he is put on death row when no one believes his ramblings about the dinosaur. If he dies, so does Adele's sister, so she must do everything in her power to save him.

Abraham Lincoln: Vampire Hunter (2010 book, 2012 movie)

Abe's sojourn into the vampiric underworld starts when he is a child, though he doesn't know it. His mother falls victim to a mysterious disease after his father stands up to his ruthless boss, Jack Barts. Even as a child, Abraham knows that Barts is somehow behind his mother's death. Once he is grown, he tries to take his revenge. To his shock, his bullets have no effect on Barts. Abe has to be rescued by a stranger whom he just met in the bar. The man calls himself Henry and tells Lincoln about how vampires are deeply involved in the slave trade as their source of food.

Abe is only interested in his own vendetta, but agrees to be a vampire hunter under Henry's guidance in order to gain the skills he needs to finally take down Barts. After hunting a series of vampires one by one, Lincoln decides he can make a much bigger difference in the world as a politician than by wielding his special silver-bladed axe. His life takes the shape of the history we know for a while, including his marriage to Mary Todd, presidential election, and the outbreak of the Civil War. But when the Southern politicians ally themselves with the vampires, unkillable soldiers start to tip the scales towards a Southern victory. Abe must confront them and the mastermind of their ascent to power.

Sherlock Holmes (2009) and *Sherlock Holmes: Game of Shadows* (2012)

I have seen some criticism about Robert Downey Jr.'s portrayal of everybody's favorite detective in this movie. Sure, Holmes plays the violin, hangs out with Dr. Watson and solves crimes in Victorian England. However, some would argue that he is missing the essence of Sherlock Holmes because he spends some of his time running around and getting blown up. I agree that Conan Doyle's Holmes was certainly subtler in his approach than this movie would make him out to be. But it is precisely this departure from the written word that makes this film Steampunk. In this first installment in the franchise, Holmes faces off against Lord Blackwell, a man who has been killing to fulfill occult rituals and appears to come back from the dead. Holmes's old flame, Irene Adler, shows up and asks him to investigate another case, but the two turn out to be intertwined.

In the second film, *Game of Shadows*, Adler reprises her appearance, but it's the famed Doctor Moriarty who drives the film. The so-called "Napoleon of Crime" is often the villain of Sherlock Holmes adaptations even though he barely factored in the source material. Watson and Mary are now married, and Holmes convinces him to complete one more case together before his faithful companion leaves the life of detective work for the comforts of home. Together, they must solve the case or see all of Europe fall into a trap that will spell war across the continent.

Sir Arthur Conan Doyle's Sherlock Holmes (2010)

Do not be fooled by the release date or the title; this is not at all the same as the Robert Downey Jr. film. As a Sherlock Holmes story, it pretty much failed miserably, but as a movie centered on futuristic technology in the Victorian era, it deserves a mention.

The movie begins when a sailing ship is taken out by a Kraken-like tentacled monster. In the next scene, we get to see a dinosaur inexplicably interrupt a rendezvous with a lady of the night. So, monsters, check. Sherlock is tortured by the fate that befell his brother, who became paralyzed after he was shot while trying to foil a bank robbery several years earlier. So, "punking" literature, check. After some watered-down deductions, Holmes and Watson find their way to a country estate where they discover the monsters are actually automatons. To top it all off, there's an aerial battle between a hot air balloon and a mechanical dragon. If you don't mind bad special effects and lackluster acting, but like silly fun, check it out.

Hansel and Gretel: Witch Hunters (2013)

In this movie's version of events, the kids are left in the forest by their birth parents for an unknown reason. They still defeat their "hostess of the grossest" but that's all just the prologue. During their struggle, they discover they should "1. never go into a house made of candy. And 2. if you are going to kill a witch, set her ass on fire." H&G also survive their encounter only because they are mysteriously immune to spells, but they don't know why.

As adults, the sibs (Jeremy Renner and Gemma Arterton) go on to become professional witch hunters. They are summoned to the town of Augsburg to investigate a spate of disappearances. The local witches are a-brewing a plot to make themselves immune to fire, and they need 12 kids to do it. In order to save the day and find out what really happened to their parents, they must face the Grand Witch and defeat her before she can carry out her dastardly plot. This one definitely fits in the category of dark but fun like *Van Helsing, Brothers Grimm,* and *Sleepy Hollow.*

Crimson Peak (2015)

This is the tale of Edith, who aspires to be a writer of Gothic fiction. As she tries to tell her potential publisher, her book is "not a ghost story. Rather, it is a story with ghosts in it." This is also an apt description of the film, and there are many clever parallels throughout.

As a female writer, she's told she must add romance in order to get the book made. But Edith doesn't let it daunt her, and she begins transcribing her manuscript using a typewriter to hide her ladylike script. The plot of the movie then follows the trajectory she is told she needs for her book. Edith is soon entangled with an impoverished baronet. After the mysterious death of her father, she decides to marry him and leave society behind. Her husband promises Edith that if he can get his invention (which is a piece of steam-powered awesomeness) running and begin mining again that all will be well. He just needs her to invest her fortune into its development. But the dead have a message for her, and she is led to clues that tell her a much more sinister story.

Steampunk Enters the Mainstream

You may not have even realized it, but Steampunk has increasingly become part of our mainstream popular culture. In addition to the films mentioned above, here are a few examples:

2010 - On the ABC television show Castle, the Steampunk fandom plays a central role in the episode called "Punked."

2011 - Justin Bieber releases a music video set in a

Steampunk-inspired Santa's workshop.

2012 - America's Next Top Model television show on the CW features a Steampunk photoshoot challenge.

2013 - Adam Lambert plays the role of "Starchild" on the Fox television show Glee. His character's identity is based on wearing Victorian-inspired attire.

2015 - Chris Hardwick, host of The Talking Dead and @Midnight appears in Steampunk clothes for a Halloween episode on Comedy Central.

2015 - The Gameshow Network airs a reality show based on themed maker challenges called Steampunk'd.

2016 - Professional wrestler Becky Lynch debuts her new Steampunk look and persona on WWE Smackdown.

Major pattern-makers now carry Steampunk lines, and if you search places like Walmart's website, you can find items listed as Steampunk.

For many fans, this is terrible news. Whether they want to preserve their own status as an "outsider" or "oddball" for liking Steampunk, or they worry about the overall quality of goods diminishing as the talent pool is "diluted," there's no denying that Steampunk is finding a larger and larger audience. But while there may be a few gatekeepers out there, for the most part, Steampunk is one of the most open and welcoming fandoms I've ever seen. People generally accept that Steampunk is so open-ended and focused on individual ideas and tastes, it is basically impossible to actually regulate who participates and how.

Which brings us right up to the present, 33 years after the term Steampunk was "born." People are fond of declaring it "dead" from time to time, but in my experience, I just see it spreading wider and wider. As the editor for Steampunk Journal and my capacity as admin for several Facebook groups, what I see is people joining in the fun more and more. Events come and go, bands form and break up, books rise and fall. But Steampunk isn't going anywhere anytime soon.

12 Popular Tropes in Steampunk: AKA Ways to Punk Your Steam

The rest of this book is composed primarily of a series of ten articles I wrote in 2015 for my first Steampunk blog, For Whom the Gear Turns. In the meantime, they've been expanded and include two new topics, and now many include some book and movie recommendations with the same theme. There may be some overlap with works I've described in the history section, but I wanted to make it possible for people to skip around and still get something out of each section on its own.

These are by no means the *only* way to "punk" the steam era or the only works out there that handle these topics, but they are some of the tried and true methods I've observed.

It is impossible to write these kinds of articles without some of my own bias coming through. I personally enjoy fiction (and by extension games, costumes, and artwork) that is rooted as much as possible in fact. I want physics to behave itself, unless there is a compelling reason for it not to. I prefer period-appropriate word choices.

This isn't to say I won't suspend my disbelief; I love fantasy and science fiction. However, I also like things to hold together logically. This can be the logic of real life, or the fantasy world being created, but consistency and thoroughness will always win out for me over sheer whimsy. I have worked in science museums and my formal training is in anthropology, so this is always at play when I approach fiction. So, there may be things about how cultures or scientific principles are presented that strike me in a way that does not bother others. In other areas, I am more than happy to simply accept what is presented and play along with a good ol' fashioned game of "what if?" But in my case, the creator has to put in the time and effort to convince me I can trust them to do it responsibly.

Feel free to use or discard the information and ideas in these pages at will, but I do hope at minimum you can find some ideas to spark your imagination and recommendations for further reading to aid in your own projects. The topics are listed alphabetically, and there may be a little overlap here and there. When applicable, I try to direct you to further discussion in other parts of the book.

For the most part, I have only included book recommendations in this volume that I have read personally. However, I have a much more comprehensive bibliography of Steampunk books on my website at www.PhoebeDarqueling.com/Steampunk-Books.

In addition, I have a page there devoted to Steampunk in movies and television. I invite you to visit these pages, and if I missed something you believe belongs on either list, please leave me a comment and I will do my best to update them.

Now, on to my twelve suggestions for punking the steam era.

12 POPULAR TROPES IN STEAMPUNK: AKA WAYS TO PUNK YOUR STEAM

Chapter 9

"Onwards and upwards," as they say, with special emphasis on *upwards* because this chapter is all about outer space.

In my meanderings through Steampunk and Victorian literature, I have run across several instances of alien contact. Invasion from a distant (or maybe not so distant) world, traveling to the stars through incredible technological advances and borrowing these advances from our "visitors" are common tropes in Steampunk literature, games, and films. I thought the best way to approach the question of how to incorporate aliens into your own project is to look at the different kinds of alien life forms that have been hypothesized in these works and what today's scientists have to say on the matter.

Scenario 1: Cephalopod Aliens (aka, Tentacles!)

One of the most famous works in classic sci-fi is, of course, *War of the Worlds* by H. G. Wells. This story was first published in 1897, and I think we can give credit to this work, as well as the Cthulhu tales of H. P. Lovecraft, for making octopuses the (un)official Steampunk mascot.

Cephalopods, such as octopuses and squid, are highly intelligent creatures, but their way of life and appearance is so foreign to us they might as well be aliens. Their intelligence gets lost behind all those creepy arms and giant, unblinking eyes. In reality, the large beasts in this family have extremely large brains for their body size, and they'd have to be smart in order to manage eight or more limbs. (I sometimes have trouble keeping track of all four of mine, so let's give credit where credit is due.)

They are also masters of camouflage, which takes an enormous amount of coordinated brain function that they do automatically. Their skin is covered in pockets of pigment they can use to change color. And their highly elastic flesh allows them to take on a variety of textures.

The pitfall with this basis for aliens is that they have extremely soft bodies and no skeletons. They need water in order to keep themselves from collapsing and are more or less useless on dry land.

But the need for water aside, cephalopods are extremely vulnerable because of their lack of armor (though the nautilus does still have a shell). The fact that they don't have a skeleton does aid them in their ability to squeeze through any crack as long as their eyes fit through, but it certainly would be a disadvantage in combat. Wells' solution was to give his betentacled aliens incredible vehicles to protect their soft bodies, and they would certainly need them.

Scenario 2: Insectoid Aliens

War of the Worlds was not the only time Wells wrote about an encounter between humans and aliens. In 1901 he wrote a story about traveling to the moon and going deep inside called *The First Men in the Moon*. The protagonists discover a vibrant and intriguing race of aliens who resemble a colony of ants gone wild and inhabit a network of tunnels that crisscross the interior. The "Selenites" have a society that is extremely segregated and specialized, and if a member's expertise is not needed, they are simply put to sleep to conserve resources. In this way, the book serves a criticism of capitalism and the Industrial Revolution that relegated laborers to a lesser status like the worker ants in a colony.

Though the Selenites resembled ants in many ways, they had soft bodies. The reduced gravitation of the moon and their cooperative society rendered the need for external armor unnecessary. In reality, insects depend on their rigid exoskeletons to keep them safe (not to mention to keep all their fluids in place.) Exoskeletons can take on a wide variety of forms and functions to suit an insect's particular niche and environment.

Because insects reproduce so quickly, they are able to undertake the natural processes of evolution much more quickly than mammals, which accounts for both their prevalence and variety on our planet, and the case would presumably be the same on other worlds. The ancestors of land-dwelling insects lived in the ancient seas of our planet and had segmented bodies. Some of these ancestors ventured onto land and they found a lush world full of plants to eat, while others remained in the sea and became today's crabs and lobsters.

The difficulty in translating an insectoid form to a large enough size to be threatening to humans is the amount of fluid that needs to be regulated in their bodies. Insects do not have blood, nor a closed circulatory system, like most of the rest of animals. They have a fluid called "hemolymph" that fills them up, but unlike blood it does not carry oxygen. Most insects actually breath through their exoskeletons, which is a throwback to when they got their oxygen from the sea.

There is a maximum size that insects can reach in our current atmospheric conditions because they simply could not get enough oxygen to their brains if they got too big. In the past, there were examples of hawk-sized dragonflies and some other extremely large insects, but this was at a time when there was more oxygen in our atmosphere. Any aliens that function like terrestrial insects would have to evolve in a highly oxygenated place (or substitute some other gas for O2), and they would still need to wear space suits just like us to survive on another planet.

Personally, what I want to see is story where a huge swarm of tiny insects are released and wreak havoc on our population. Or perhaps some kind of predatory pet of the intelligent race. Sure, they wouldn't have built the spacecraft themselves, so there would have to be a primary alien race that is separate from them, but can you imagine the devastation they could bring? Too often I see depictions of aliens and alien planets with only a single race of beings, but if our incredibly interconnected world is anything to go on, there would be myriad species on any planet in order for ecosystems to flourish.

Scenario 3: Humanoid aliens

This is probably the form that aliens most often take in popular science fiction. The inhabitants of the alien worlds of *Star Trek* and *Star Wars,* for instance, are almost always four-limbed, one-headed, and bipedal. They express themselves using vocal language more often than not, but sometimes have telepathic abilities or employ sign language that they convey with their five-fingered hands.

In some ways, this portrayal comes out of our tendency to assume that human beings are the "most highly evolved" species on our planet, so other intelligent species elsewhere must look like us. Evolutionary scientists tend not to use this term, preferring instead to refer to the degree of derivation, i.e. how much a species has changed from its ancestors. In this way, humans are certainly highly derived, but we are by no means the pinnacle of "progress."

One advantage of using a humanoid shape is that it allows a creator an opportunity to draw parallels between the human race and other aliens. The more alike we are, but at the same time giving them key cultural, social, and physical differences allows for interesting commentary and situations.

For instance, in Garrett P. Serviss's unauthorized and heavily edited adaptation of *War of the Worlds* set in the United States entitled *Fighters from Mars,* the Martians are human shaped. However, in a nod to the different conditions on the red planet, they are giants. In the sequel, *Edison's Conquest of Mars*, human fighters visit our neighboring world in order to strike back before the Martians can regroup. They find that the aliens abducted humans several centuries earlier and have been using them as slave labor. This is the first instance of both space suits and alien abduction in literature.

However, walking on two feet is not the most stable means of transport. If you think about it, the only thing more tippable than a person is a person standing on one leg, and the animals such as snails that only have one "foot" are actually highly stable and have no trouble getting around. Luckily (or rather, evolutionarily) for us we have five toes on each foot which aids our ability to balance.

What a bipedal lifestyle does offer us is the freedom to use our dexterous hands to manipulate objects and build amazing structures. Which begs the question, is there really any reason to stop at just one pair of hands. What about an alien species with eight limbs? That would give them the stability of a quadruped plus four hands to explore their world.

In *The Amber Spyglass*, the third book in Phillip Pullman's "His Dark Materials" series, we see something in this ballpark. He creates an alien race that has six limbs, two of which they use to hold onto a round seed pod. This makes them like the axle of a car. The other four limbs are used to propel the creatures forward. In many landscapes, adopting wheel-dependent transport wouldn't make any sense. To make things all hang together, Pullman uses the device that volcanic eruptions created natural roadways for the inhabitants to use. Their relationship with the seed pods is symbiotic, because their hard shells are difficult to crack. Using them as wheels eventually breaks the pods open, and the creatures plant the seeds and tend to the mother trees, much like some species of ants in the rain forest.

What do Scientists Think?

One of the prevailing theories in regards to the prospects of contact from another world has a lot of potential in Steampunk. Many believe that because of the dangers of space travel and the great distances that would need to be covered, our first contact will more than likely be with a machine from another planet, not a biological being. I would love to read a story about an encounter between Vic-Wardians and a super advanced computer or automaton from outer space! There is a lot of potential here just waiting to be explored.

Chapter 10

This chapter is mostly for the benefit of aspiring writers and filmmakers and focuses on how to make things feel authentic in a work of altered history and a few areas where alterations can be found in other works. For information about using the future rather than the past for your Steampunk setting, look to the "Make it Futuristic" chapter. And for a discussion on the logistics and consequences of time travel, check out "Make it Travel Through Time."

I went to my very first convention, Marscon, in 2014. It was more of a general interest fest with lots of different kinds of geekery, but there were a few seminars aimed at Steampunks. The best one I attended was called "Alternate History and the History of Time" and the speakers addressed ways to make an alternate history feel authentic.

One of the audience members posed the question, "What is the best way to let my readers know about the time period and my alterations to it?" And the entire panel agreed that good writers show their audiences what they want them to know, they don't tell them outright.

When it comes to altered history, the process is two-fold. First, you need to make sure that the readers know, at least roughly, what year it is. But second, and really more importantly, you need them to understand that the world of your story, game, or film is somehow different without a bulky piece of exposition laying it all out for them.

Show, Don't Tell

The best writers and filmmakers never just tell their readers anything, they seduce us into reading more. (Games are a different story, see below). With seduction comes a certain air of anticipation, tantalizing tidbits dropped here and there to intrigue and draw us deeper into the truth the creators are striving to reveal. Sure, you could have a prologue that lays out where the timeline got altered in detail, but this takes a lot of the artistry out of the process and may serve to actually drive some readers away.

For instance, a person close to me, let's call her Liz, exclusively reads two different types of books: mysteries and historical fiction. Her tastes are grounded in things that really did happen, or at least seem like they really could have happened. If Liz picked up a book and was immediately told the steps that lead to a vastly different state of the world, she'd put it right back down. Despite my tutelage, she has very little interest in the genres of science fiction and fantasy (though she did enjoy *Firefly* after we got a few episodes in), and would be totally turned off by this sledgehammer-like approach. Liz is the type of consumer who would need to first be introduced to characters that she could care about to draw her in and a compelling story to keep her reading even if stuff started to get "weird."

"Well, maybe I'm not writing a book for Liz!" you may be thinking. Fair enough. There are plenty of die-hard sci-fi and fantasy fans out there who could be interested in your subject no matter how it is presented. Maybe that is enough for you. I know I read and watch a lot of things strictly because they fit into the Steampunk oeuvre, but I wouldn't necessarily recommend them to someone who isn't already interested in it.

And let's face it, Steampunk is gaining in popularity, so in general the audience for such works is growing. However, I'd say the best way to succeed as a creator is to bring new people into the fold. This means crafting something objectively good that would appeal to people even if they are the uninitiated.

Games, on the other hand, do benefit from laying all their cards on the table at the get-go, but that is because the act of playing is where the seduction occurs. To succeed in the world of a game, a player needs to understand the mechanics of gameplay in addition to the story line. This often comes from practice by playing the game itself. As the player gets better at manipulating the world of the creator and navigating it successfully, they will be drawn ever deeper into that world.

Role-players and tabletop gamers are seduced by the act of participation, which can keep them coming back and wanting more. They are actively involved in the act of creation as they build characters and alliances, which is different from being the passive receptor during a good book.

Do Your Homework

No one should attempt to write an alternate history story without having a good working knowledge of the actual history they are messing with. Many readers would probably miss anachronisms, but there are a lot of people who know their history and would be bothered by attitudes or expressions that have no place in that time. If you aren't the researcher type, you may be better suited creating a fantasy world rather than attempting to punk the past.

If you are going to include anachronisms as part of your "punking" scheme, make sure that they fit in logically with the other alterations you are making to the timeline. You must be purposeful with this tactic, or the trolls will come out and attack you for a lack of authenticity. I found a great reference book called *Hustlers, Harlots, and Heroes* that I use to inform my own writing, and there lots of other books out there to help to add details that make your story ring true.

Below are just a few suggestions to get you started, but the best way to figure out how to show your time period is to *know* your time period. Knowing your stuff will also make it easier to implement the "show, don't tell" method of drawing in your audience.

There are plenty of noteworthy events that an author can reference instead of explicitly naming the year. For instance, there were several international exhibitions during the steam era, and a passing mention of a new technology that was unveiled at one or the inventor behind it can give a reader a touchstone. Or you can focus on landmarks, such as the completion of Tower Bridge. If you know that you want to situate your story late in Victoria's reign, you could have a character consider attending the opening of the Albert Memorial.

The status of wars or diplomacy work great as well. Soldiers returning home after the second Anglo-Afghan war could be spotted in a cafe and noted in passing. Many writers turn to referencing literature and authors to give at least a rough idea of when their story is taking place. Someone could start their morning by reading a story in the newspaper about the first lighter than air flight and reflect on how technology was changing the world.

There are also famous figures who can be integrated into your plot line. Charles Darwin, for instance, is well-known far beyond Steampunk circles. Adding in a reference to him making a personal appearance or perhaps a passing acquaintance with a character places your story before his death in 1882. Authors, poets, explorers, inventors, scientists, or even the sinister Jack the Ripper can do a lot to situate your story in time. In the graphic novels, *The Thrilling Adventures of Lovelace and Babbage* (2015), these two famous figures team up to fight crime using their analytical engine.

Maybe one of your characters is a fan of The Strand magazine and is feeling devastated by the untimely death of Sherlock Holmes. Or, perhaps they get pulled into the action of your story while on their way to purchase the latest volume of poetry by Algernon Charles Swinburne. A person could have very strong feelings about a politician running for election, or engage in a debate about the benefits of alternating current.

This kind of approach can do a lot to add the flavor of the time and place without hitting an audience over the head with it.

Think It Through

History is complex, so if you choose to alter some element of it there may be a widespread ripple effect. For instance, in the world of Gail Carriger's Parasol Protectorate series, supernatural beings have been fully integrated into society. The good queen Vic has both a werewolf and a vampire advisor to help her navigate this unique political situation, and they have a distinct place in the social structure of the United Kingdom, which differs from the way they are viewed in other parts of the world. In *Whitechapel Gods* (2008) by S.M. Peters, there are competing quasi-religious factions that enforce the will of very real gods who have taken over the social and political systems of London. The future is forever altered in *The Difference Engine* (1990) because computers become viable much earlier than in real life.

These are all suitably large changes to create real differences in the fabric the era in which they occur, and are great examples of alternate histories with rich back stories.

On the other hand, you can write a much smaller story. Alternate histories don't have to completely break the time period they are depicting and reshape the world. One of my absolute favorite television shows is *Murdoch Mysteries*, and the writers do an elegant job of presenting the main character as just slightly ahead of his time in a very realistic way. The detective piggy-backs on the existing science of the 1890s and creates methods of collecting evidence and catching the culprits without causing any type of large-scale change to society.

In Steampunk, you can also find examples of taking real historical events but changing the reasons behind them. *Abraham Lincoln: Vampire Hunter*, for instance, started with a historical figure with a well-known history, but found ways to put his actions in to a very different and darker narrative. This approach means that there doesn't need to be much of a ripple effect, because you aren't actually changing the major events of history, they are just being recontextualized.

Regressive vs. Progressive

Broadly speaking, alternative histories usually stem from something happening earlier than it did in real life, or from something *not* happening the way it really did; if this or that world power won or lost certain wars, for instance.

You may then be presented with that altered past, or a present and/or future that was shaped by the happening or non-happening. Depending on the nature of said event, the result could be a world that is regressive or progressive according to our real present.

The steam era had plenty of wonders, but it also had plenty of ills. In a regressive take on alternative history, these ills persist or may have become even more pronounced. This often swings these stories into the realm of dystopia that serve as a warning. For instance, the Victorian era saw an unprecedented amount of wealth disparity. Some changes to history could see this persist and continue to grow. We know much more about how diseases spread and how to treat illnesses now than in the past, but a little tweak here or there and these things could have gone undiscovered for a long time. Many types of social reforms occurred during this era as well, such as the abolition of slavery. A regressive alternative history could see this practice still alive and well. The authors who were working closest to the Cyberpunk era when the word Steampunk was born tend to have a bleaker outlook on the world and often chose to explore these more regressive what ifs.

On the other hand, contemporary Steampunk tends to go in the other direction. As our own world becomes more inclusive, so do alternative histories. People across the gender spectrum are starting to make appearances. For example, *Spectral City* (2018) by Leanna Renee Hieber and the Showtime show *Penny Dreadful* both include transgender characters. Though the Victorian era has a reputation for being repressed and buttoned-up, this really wasn't the case. Many Steampunk works embrace a variety of romantic and sexual relationships which are in reality completely on point for the era but seem strange because of our miseducation.

Characters with different kinds of physical or mental constraints are also starting to find a home in the imagined past. Sometimes, this is through the use of intricate clockwork prostheses, but not always. Blind, deaf, and mute characters are increasingly making appearances, as are characters with a range of strengths and weaknesses brought on by how their brain is wired. Post-traumatic stress disorder and other types of both anxiety and depression find expressions in Steampunk. If you are interested in a collection of short stories that center on differently abled characters in a Steampunk setting, check out *Steampunk Universe*.

The eccentric genius is a popular character type in both scientific romances and later science fiction. More than likely, some of the people who made the greatest technological leaps also lived with something we would consider "mental illness" today. Nikola Tesla, for instance, has habits and behaviors that are well documented and very odd, yet he is one of the great thinkers of the era. So, it only seems right that we start to see more of this.

People of color and women who helped shape the steam era are also being recognized and incorporated. For example, in *The Frankenstein Chronicles* show, they (historically accurately) have a police officer of African descent in the cast. In the past, even a decade ago, viewers would be perfectly happy to see white-washed version of the past. But more and more people are demanding representation for minorities in their art.

The irony here is that these people all existed in the real past, but because they were largely left out of the narrative, adding them is now is a form of "punking" what has come before. So, as an extension of the idea that you must do your homework, don't only focus on the big events. Make sure to take a look at the social and cultural things going on at the moment you want to change the time line and incorporate some variation in your story to help give it more depth and interest.

For a more in-depth discussion of incorporating women into your Steampunk, check out the next chapter, "Make it Feminist." For more information about integrating people of color and different cultures, see "Make it Multicultural."

Chapter 11

For many of us living today, it can seem ridiculous to consider that half of the population was denied the right to vote because of their plumbing, but the suffrage movement was considered radical in its day. There is an excellent display of photos, paraphernalia and accounts by British suffragettes at the Museum of London. During a visit in 2014, I gained a real appreciation for the violent opposition they faced for something that we now take totally as a given. Feminism of course transcends the right to vote, but equality between the sexes (and/or all along the gender spectrum) is the underpinning of it all.

Put it to the Test

You've probably heard of the Bechdel Test, but in case you haven't, here's the skinny. Alison Bechdel wrote a comic strip in 1985 that featured two women discussing movies. One tells the other that she never sees a movie unless it satisfies three criteria: There are at least two female characters, who talk to each other, and their conversation must be about something other than a man (any man, it doesn't have to be romantic). Later versions also include that the female characters must have names, and there are of course some biases here against settings or storylines where female characters wouldn't work in the narrative, but it is the baseline often studied by statisticians.

It should also be noted that just because a work of fiction passes this test, that does not make it inherently feminist. There can still be an overall misogynist message or scenes that degrade women whether or not they pass this simple test. The point is that the test is incredibly bare bones and it is still difficult to pass. It turns out this is actually incredibly hard to find in most Hollywood films, and books and television don't fare much better. Let's take these criteria one by one.

Criteria #1

First, there must be at least two female characters. It is so difficult to find anything that even satisfies this simple first step. I have noticed in several movies and books that there will be a nod to womankind in the form of a single female in a sea of male faces, and she is often the smartest or kick-assingest one in the cast. In the movie *9*, for instance, there are sentient dolls that are totally gender neutral to look at, but one of them has a female voice actor behind it. This is the doll that takes action and performs acts of derring-do. Hermione Granger is the bright one in the *Harry Potter* trio, and Leeloo from *The Fifth Element* is engineered to be a perfect being.

This is of course better than having no female characters at all, or falling into the timeworn pattern of the early days of film-making where women are only there to be rescued by the male heroes. But I still find this kind of tokenism problematic. In a way, these characters are given special abilities or power in order to justify their presence in the story, because just being a human isn't enough. They have to be made somehow exceptional or they are not welcome to join "the boys' club."

In *The League of Extraordinary Gentlemen* film, for instance, Mina Murray is the only woman in the league (which of course, carries the word gentlemen in the title) and filmmakers thought it was necessary to make her a vampire. I can't say for certain if this was merely for the sake of adding a more cinematic bent to the character or in order to give her some specialness to earn her place in the group, but it struck me as the latter. This is a deviation from the books, where Mina is not only the team leader, but she does so by force of personality and is a completely ordinary human being.

Criteria #2

Next up, the two female characters must talk to each other. I call this one "The Bond Girl Paradox." Almost every spy movie features at least a few female characters in the story. They may be heroes or villains, they are nearly always hyper-sexualized, and may even be smart or good at their jobs to boot. But they never overlap. They only interact with the central male figure, but rarely occupy the same space, and even if they do, their focus is totally on the James Bond character. (I'm looking at you, Moneypenny.)

Again, this is a step in the right direction, but still puts the man at the very center of the story. This occurs in lots of films, books, and TV shows, but I can only think of one movie I have ever seen where a series of beautiful men are throwing themselves into the path of a central female character, and that was Barbarella circa 1968. The "reverse-harem" is a trend in romance novels these days, so perhaps we will start seeing it in visual media as well.

Criteria #3

And now, the last step: These two women must be discussing something other than a man. I admit, I do find this slightly problematic because taken to its furthest extent, to meet this criterion would mean to cut out half of the world's population as a subject of discourse. However, it isn't actually difficult to overcome and pass this simple test because it only has to be *one exchange* in the entire work.

In real life, women have jobs, hobbies, and friends that they talk about. Some enjoy discussing sports, others brew their own beer or go on wine tasting trips. My mother-in-law and I went on a quest to try all of the breakfast joints in her town, and I have sisters-in-law who make their own paper or spend free time practicing calligraphy. I have spent days on end with dozens women as part of wedding festivities. Only a few sentences here and there had anything to do with significant others or one's relationship status.

Besides giving a character something to talk about, hobbies

and interests add depth to people and more interest to scenes. In Blake Snyder's *Save the Cat!* book about screenwriting, he advises that the main character should have at least "six things that need fixing." The degree of difficulty should vary, and maybe they don't all get solved. It's a great shorthand way to think about characterization and adding interest to characters you create.

In the Victorian era, your female characters may be more limited in the types of employment that they could have than today's women, but that doesn't mean they wouldn't have interests and hobbies. Before television, people read extensively, supported the arts, joined organizations like The Temperance League and volunteered through their churches. They had opinions, sometimes totally biased due to misinformation or culture in which they live (and isn't that fascinating?), and they would discuss them with gusto.

Female Steampunk Archetypes

As discussed in the "Make it Alternative" chapter, the act of "punking" the past is difficult. Change things too much, and it feels like the creator didn't do their homework. Change too little, and they can be accused of "glorifying" a troubled past.

In black and white science fiction and adventure films, it's fairly common to have a token female character who is the "plucky reporter." This archetype is born of the desire to have a female character (who does often end up being the love interest), but needing a period-appropriate reason for her to be present. As a job that can be viewed as one-part secretary and one-part gossip, being a journalist was a suitable job for women of that era. Sometimes, there are female researchers or scientists, though they are often the daughter of the male head scientist as their "in."

In the same way, Steampunk has developed some of its own archetypes for empowering women, but without straying so far out of historical bounds to be completely anachronistic and distracting. Here are a few I've seen.

The Angsty Aristocrat

In short, no one puts baby in the corner. These are the women of means who rebel against their gilded cages. They often refuse to marry who they are supposed to. They are sick and tired (or just bored) of their current existence and seek adventure. She wants passion and a way to shake herself out of her placid existence. She just might consider wearing a pair of trousers, but more than likely her fine bustled gowns and elaborate hairdos are going to be the norm.

The Private Detective/Problem Solver

This is often an offshoot of the Angsty Aristocrat. Affluent women in the steam era were known for their commitment to charitable works, but this archetype goes beyond writing a check and gets her hands dirty. More than likely, she's got at least one set of men's clothes in order to help her sneak out of the house and avoid detection. She uses her connections and wealth to help the downtrodden or get to the bottom of a mysterious disappearance of a peer or loved one. Chances are, what she finds much more than she bargained for, and becomes embroiled in a conspiracy. She may work on the quiet or have an established role, such as a police matron, but the men around her will not be supportive of her efforts.

The Tinker Girl

Much like the aforementioned "plucky reporter," the Tinker Girl likes to understand how the world works and isn't afraid to ask questions. Most often, if you try to get her into a dress, you'll have a fight on your hands. She will more than likely have some kind of goggles to help protect her while she does her metalworking. She is rebellious and stubborn, and usually thinks she's smarter or more knowledgeable than she really is and gets herself into trouble. There's a good chance her father is an inventor and she grew up without a mother present, much like the female researcher of the 1950s films.

The Spinster Scholar

I use the term "spinster" here loosely because in the Victorian era, one only had to reach the ripe old age of 25 to start having that label applied. What's important about this archetype is that her work (whatever it may be) is much more important to her than anything else. She eschews what society expects of her and does not give any real thought to having a family. She does not care at all for fashion, but also just wants to be left alone so isn't going to go out of her way to rock the boat. Oftentimes, she has some kind of elaborate pair of spectacles or goggles to help her with her research, which may be scientific or supernatural in nature.

The Airship Captain/Adventurer

If the world of your Steampunk story involves airships, there's more than likely going to be at least one female captain. She may or may not be accepted by her male counterparts, but more than likely she will be because her crew will be composed of men and they defer to her. If she is a side character, the main character is usually unsure if she can be trusted, and as often as not, she turns out to be a villain. If she is the main character, she'll be brave and physically fit, and eschew the annoyance of dealing with skirts flapping in the wind for the comfort of trousers and a long coat. However, she'll still probably have a corset (most likely made of leather) that she'll wear on the outside. Flight goggles are a given.

Feminism Means Equality

So far in this chapter, I have only been focusing on women and how they are treated in fictional works. The term "feminist," however, has a broader reach than celebrating those bearing female organs. There is still the common misconception that to be a feminist is to be categorically anti-male, but this is not the case. There may be individuals who feel this way due to resenting the status quo and those who do not recognize the inherent inequality. However, as a philosophy, feminism has to do with treating everyone equally regardless of their gender, to treat every human being as a human being. This includes men.

Note that I said "gender" rather than "sex." As the conversation surrounding different gender identities expands, so does the pool of individuals that feminism is advocating for. There are many ways to be marginalized according to how we look, how we love, and how we live. Things are better now than they were in the steam era, but there is still plenty of room for improvement.

I do not mean to say that everyone's plight or solutions are going to be exactly the same. As a cisgender (meaning my gender identity matches what I was assigned to at birth) white female from the suburbs, I am not going to have the same problems as a transgender black male. Or even a cisgender white male, for that matter. Our society has different expectations for all identities, and these expectations can be toxic. At its core, feminism seeks to call attention to these harmful discrepancies and asks for equality across the board. The goal is for everyone to be able to be exactly who they are and be treated with the respect afforded to all.

Our Steampunk creations give us the opportunity to extend this ideal into the real and imagined past.

Chapter 12

MAKE IT FUNNY

I read once that in every survey when men and women are asked what trait they find most attractive in a potential mate, both sexes agree that a "good sense of humor" is the key to their hearts. But one time, the researchers asked them what that meant to them, and the answer was very interesting.

For the most part, female responders said that an ideal potential partner "makes me laugh," while males tended to say they were looking for "someone who laughs at my jokes." Personally, I know I exhibit more a "groaner" type humor that relies heavily on puns, so getting even a snicker out of someone is a real treat. Here's an example:

Vendor at a convention: We make all of our goggles by hand.

Me: Wow, you must have a lot of special tools.

Trader: I just got this new one for punching holes in the straps so I can make them customized for each buyer. It is a big time saver. I used to have to sit for like an hour using an awl for each pair.

Me: Ugh, awl-ful.

Bu-dum ching!

Yep, I know, that was bad. But what can I say? Puns tickle my brain.

Humor is Subjective

Humor is a funny thing (nudge, nudge), and what makes one person snicker could easily make someone else angry. For instance, my mother has started writing plays for her local theater community, and she recently had a very strange experience when it came to getting her work approved for performance. The show is an interactive murder mystery that features "Hemlock Holmes," a parody of Doyle's Great Detective. He's on a retreat on an American riverboat, so the story takes place during the steam era we all love so much.

Rather than voting to approve her work, she was sent a list of a dozen jokes from the show that the committee deemed "offensive." This included the one that I thought was the hands-down funniest one in the entire show. Was it offensive? Okay, a bit. But the word choice was also technically period-appropriate. Plus, the parody form of theater is meant to be a bit cheeky. Here's the joke, I'll let you choose for yourself:

A fortune-telling midget is arrested for murder, but then escapes.

CHAPTER 12

The headlines read: Small medium at large!

The whole situation got me thinking about the difficulty of working humor into a story, especially one set in a different time period. As stoical as folks all look in the old-timey photos, we know that the people of Regency and Victorian periods lived rich, full, and probably often humorous lives. We're talking about the period that gave birth to Vaudeville and stand-up comedians, burlesque acts, and comic strips. "Laughing gas" (yep, the same stuff the dentist gives you nowadays) was a favorite recreational drug among the upper crust at the beginning of the 19th century, and circus clowns as we know them today came into being. So, despite the perception of stuffy morality of the Victorian period, their stiff upper lips were most definitely quivering with laughter some of the time.

So, What Did the Victorians Find Funny?

During my research I found out about an amazing website called The Dictionary of Victorian London. Among other things, the author, Jackson Lee, posts and tweets Victorian era jokes. Here are a few of my personal favorites:

"See here, waiter, I've found a button in my salad." "That's all right, sir, it's part of the dressing."

Marriage is an institution intended to keep women out of mischief and get them into trouble.

Why should the number 288 never be mentioned in company? Because it is two gross.

Pawnbrokers prefer customers without any redeeming qualities.

These are all pretty innocuous, but there are also plenty of examples out there of jokes that are racist and misogynistic. In America, the "coon" caricature of African-born people was ubiquitous in the 1800s and advertisers co-opted their dialect (which reflected their enforced lack of education) as a novelty to sell advertising. Chinese immigrants and native Americans were also stereotyped and used in the same way. While historically accurate, these are examples of marginalizing people and also profiting by that marginalization in a way that Civil Rights activists have worked hard to dismantle.

Thinning Skin: Good or Bad?

Recently, *The Atlantic Monthly* ran two extremely interesting articles that I feel relate to the topic of the perils of trying to incorporate humor into your work of fiction. Both of them focused on college campuses and the repercussions of going overboard when it comes to being politically correct, both in Academia and in entertainment. The Coddling of the American Mind, by Greg Lukianoff and Jonathan Haidt, had some interesting insights about how our culture has swung so far towards ostensibly protecting every single minority's rights that the very nature of going to college has been changed:

"The press has typically described these developments as a resurgence of political correctness. That's partly right, although there are important differences between what's happening now and what happened in the 1980s and '90s. That movement sought to restrict speech (specifically hate speech aimed at marginalized groups), but it also challenged the literary, philosophical, and historical canon, seeking to widen it by including more-diverse perspectives. The current movement is largely about emotional well-being. More than the last, it presumes an extraordinary fragility of the collegiate psyche, and therefore elevates the goal of protecting students from psychological harm. The ultimate aim, it seems, is to turn campuses into "safe spaces" where young adults are shielded from words and ideas that make some uncomfortable. And more than the last, this movement seeks to punish anyone who interferes with that aim, even accidentally."

This argument is interesting, but also misses an underlying truth. People only take risks when they feel secure. I know, that sounds counter-intuitive. However, it is also true. To overcome the "fight or flight" response to danger, we have to perceive the danger as something we can overcome. When we head off for college, there's plenty to be scared of already. The goal of making everyone feel welcome and secure enough to take risks is not, in itself, a terrible goal.

The other article, which applies the most to the topic of humor was called That's Not Funny! Every year, the careers of aspiring comedians are put on the line when they attempt to get on the college circuit. There is an annual showcase for universities of all sizes to choose entertainers for the coming year. The problem is that these acts have to become so incredibly sterilized in order for the comedians to book gigs that they feel they are no longer funny. Or the funniest people don't get jobs because something they said was perceived as maybe being possibly offensive to even a single student.

The goal of being inclusive is, of course, admirable, and discrimination is bad. At the same time, comedy has the capacity to make us think, to change our perceptions and see things from a different perspective. But only if we let it.

So How Does This All Relate to Steampunk?

There are some people who do not like Steampunk because they feel it romanticizes an era where discrimination and inequality ran rampant. And it is true, most people were uneducated, lived in poverty, and led short, brutal lives. Things we take for granted such as germ theory and basic nutrition were still not fully understood. However, I'd say that the best Steampunk out there does not glorify these things, rather it forces readers and viewers to confront these realities in our past (or create alternative, sometimes contrary expressions of the past) and deal with them. And a great way to soften that blow can be through humor.

I think it important for readers and writers alike to remember that they do not have to like every character in a story. Frankly, universally likable people are boring. The characters who populate a world can and should be biased by their upbringings and blind to other points of view. Like real humans, they should make mistakes, have slips of the tongue and have deeply held though totally unproven beliefs. And if some of these foibles get them into trouble, which leads to character development and growth, everyone wins.

Jokes made by these unlikable characters, or a likable character in a moment of weakness or naivete, are a perfect opportunity to confront some of the issues of inequality I mentioned. These are the comments that cause a sharp intake of breath or a few moments of a slack jaw in an audience. Like a little whap to the side of the head, they get our attention and make our minds reel. It also gives other characters a chance to respond, thus offering a platform for a different point of view.

CHAPTER 12

A Funny Thing Happened on the Way to the Vivisection

Then again, maybe that's not your style. I have run across several works of Steampunk that are delightfully funny and have very little to do with social commentary, or at least not in a soapbox kind of way. Rather than getting our feathers ruffled about the way things were in the past, we can also decide to find the humor in the ridiculousness. People in the steam era used cuttlefish in their toothpaste, prescribed orgasm to treat a woman's "wandering womb," and thought that bathing was bad for one's health. They owned special clothes just for driving and women's bathing suits required black woolen socks. There is a big capacity for embracing the weird and wacky world of the Victorians and hopefully your readers will be willing to go along for the ride.

Another approach could be to do a mash-up of the era with our own. Applying contemporary sensibilities and situations to the past is a great opportunity to point out how ludicrous it really was. A great example of this is the film *A Million Ways to Die in the West* (2014). The protagonist is a shepherd in the old west, and he absolutely hates everything about that time and place.

Let's Get Something Straight

More than likely, the comedy you will want to work into your Steampunk project will be in the form of dialogue. The tried and true method for these interactions is to have one "clown" and one "straight man" (or woman). The various antics of the clown are augmented by the straight man's reactions, which can range from total serious detachment to anger. Your combo could be a servant/master, a hero/sidekick, siblings, husband and wife, or any other combination of two people you want. The straight man's job is most often to represent society at large, while the clown (also called "the banana man" or "comedian") is there to transgress it.

The moniker "clown" may put you in mind of a buffoon, but this half of the duo doesn't necessarily need to be stupid or slow. I saw a great example of this dynamic in a Steampunk setting at Edinburgh Fringe Festival in 2014. There was a fantastic magical act called Morgan and West, and while both men performed amazing acts of prestidigitation, one is clearly acting as the straight man.

Usually, it's the clown who gets all the laughs, but not always. In *Jeeves and Wooster*, for instance, it is usually Jeeves (Stephen Fry) who uses his droll delivery to elicit the chuckles, while his charge Bertie Wooster (Hugh Laurie) bumbles through life and occasionally sings a silly song. Wooster is definitely the clown in the pair, but is not funnier than the straight man.

You also don't need to commit to an arrangement for the duration of a whole novel if you don't want. Characters have moods, and circumstances change, so your duo may not be in comedic place in the story every step of the way. Your clowns can also be fleeting members of your cast of characters. In my own works, I have used a few different "clowns" who interact with various members of my core group of characters so they serve the purpose of a foil, but I also don't have to keep them around any longer than I need to for their primary purpose (exposition, lightening the mood, etc.).

Take the excerpt from my first novel, *Riftmaker* below, for example.

"Really, it was all I could do to convince Uncle that I should be moving out at all."

CHAPTER 12

"Why yes," said Tina as she reached for a meringue, "he may have to resort to holding a gala every night to entice you back. Tragic really." Her eyes twinkled with possibilities.

"Oh, please don't suggest it! My feet and my dressmakers can hardly keep up as it is."

"Then I suppose it's a good thing you are going." Tina popped the tart into her mouth and continued with her mouth full. "Imagine the scandal if your feet fell off during a party. Uncle would never live it down."

Olivia smiled and added two lumps of sugar to her porcelain cup. "Unfortunately for the rest of you, someone would probably declare it the newest trend, and you would all be expected to cut yours off, too."

"Fashion is fickle; I'll give you that." Tina poured the tea. "So, speaking of scandal, we didn't get a chance to talk last night after your rendezvous. I've been dying to know what happened." Alarm gripped her stomach, and Olivia looked around for fear of being overheard, but the servants had already completely vacated the garden. Tina followed her cousin's gaze, then waved away her concern. "What, them? They wouldn't say anything even if they did hear."

"I'm not so sure about that," Olivia murmured.

"I've been getting you into trouble for years, and not one of your staff has ever tattled on us. What's different now?" Tina peered at Olivia over the brim of her cup as she blew off the steam.

"I don't know." She shrugged. "Maybe because the stakes are higher than a broken cookie jar?"

"When you're six, the stakes don't get much higher," Tina said, adding her habitual giggle.

The scene goes on for several more pages, but after this encounter the readers won't see Tina again until the end of the book. I try to use her first as a foil for Olivia (who the reader has only just met) and later to facilitate exposition, but I don't have to make a commitment to her as a character, or her brand of frivolity, for the duration.

And of course, you don't have to use this method. Characters could riff off each other just as easily as they can act as foils. There must be some reason these people are spending time together, and it probably has something to do with feeling the other has a good sense of humor.

When I was researching this chapter, I asked my husband whom he thought was funnier out of the two of us. He said it was probably me, and maybe he's right. I do make a lot more overt attempts at humor, which often takes the form of me mumbling something punny under my breath for only him to hear. For my part, I think he's very funny, especially when people mistake his deadpan delivery for a serious remark. But so often we are playing off one another it is difficult to really make that judgment call.

Recommendations

Here are a few Steampunk, Weird West, and Victorian works that I hope will make you laugh. Many of these have been discussed in detail in other parts of this book.

Letters Between Gentlemen by Professor Elemental and Nimue Brown

"Parasol Protectorate" series by Gail Carriger

"Ichabod Temperance" series by Ichabod Temperance

No Rest for the Wicked by Phoebe Darqueling
The General (1926)
Blazing Saddles (1974)
The Importance of Being Earnest (2002) (also a play)
A Muppet Christmas Carol (1992)
Muppet Treasure Island (1996)
Wild, Wild West (1999)
A Million Ways to Die in the West (2014)

Conclusion

I started off this chapter with some bad puns, so it only seems appropriate to end with some too. Here's a recreation of a real conversation my husband and I had the other day when we sighted longhorn sheep in the Badlands.

Him: It looks like the sheep are all leaving. I guess they are sick of getting their picture taken.

Me: You'd think they'd be "ewe-sed" to it by now, wouldn't you?

Him: Perhaps they are on the "lamb."

Me: They could just be feeling "sheepish." Or they've had enough, and they are collectively throwing up their hooves and saying "baa-humbug."

Him: That really gets my goat.

Me: I bet they "herd" us coming.

Him: Don't worry, they'll be back. They are just "kid-ding" around.

Me: Oof, that one was "baaaaad."

Whether that made you guffaw or groan, go forth and infuse your Steampunk meanderings with your own sense of humor. We could all use a good laugh.

Chapter 13

MAKE IT FUTURISTIC

Bringing the Future into the Past
The early movers and shakers in what we now call "science fiction" set the stage for contemporary authors to dream big when it comes to the kinds of technology one could find in the 18th, 19th, and early 20th centuries. Jules Verne brought us the electricity driven Nautilus. H. G. Wells took readers to the moon. Mary Shelley woke the dead. And R. L. Stevenson introduced a concoction that let out Dr. Jekyll's dark side, just to name a few.

CHAPTER 13

Technological innovations were being developed at an incredible rate, and these new innovations had a deep impact on society. Science fiction grew out of a natural tendency to ask "what if?" and to project the effects of these changes into the future. Steampunk authors also do this, but the "future" is often in their own past. With the benefit of both hindsight and foresight, they can draw from the world of early science fiction, as well as from their own lives, to create interesting twists on the Industrial Revolution and the greater implications of the Age of Enlightenment.

The Age of Enlightenment (aka The Age of Reason or just The Enlightenment) spanned the mid-1600s to the late 1700s. Due to innovations in printing technology the century before, philosophers like Sir Francis Bacon and Renee Descartes, as well as scientists such as Sir Isaac Newton, were able to share their ideas with unprecedented speed. Literacy was spreading, due in a large part to the use of the vernacular in both religious and popular texts.

As printing technology improved during the Industrial Revolution, moving from hand crank operated to steam-powered, it became less expensive, and the demand continued to grow. This, in turn, lead to an explosion of writing, both fiction and non-fiction, and its subsequent consumption on a mass scale.

The world would not see such a leap in communication capabilities again until the World Wide Web arrived in 1989 (the "internet" was invented 20 years earlier but did not offer access to the average person). It should come as no surprise that Steampunk also came into being around the same time, drawing from the past to inform the present and the future.

One popular trope in Steampunk literature is the introduction of fully functioning automatons. They are often at the behest of the forces of evil and the heroes must overcome a foe (or in many cases an army) that is practically immortal. Some are run solely on clockwork or steam power, and others are an amalgamation of biological and mechanical elements. Anyone reading these works is aware that this kind of technology has never come to be even centuries later, but that doesn't stop it from being an interesting game of "what if?"

In the case of automatons, the creators are taking something that has never happened and put it into an earlier time. In other instances, they may only be taking liberties with a few decades. It only takes a clever character (with the right funds and circumstances) to take technology that was really available during their time and modify it to fit a need. Like the use of sonar in *Murdoch Mysteries* for instance, or using one your characters as the first to create an innovation that we already have a basis for in history.

A good example of the latter is the world of *The Difference Engine*, where the completion highly sophisticated computers leads to something resembling the internet centuries before it really came to be. The "futuristic" technology cannot help but have a large impact on society, and the authors carry the implications to a logical conclusion.

Bringing the Past into the Future

Another genre of science fiction that sometimes dovetails with Steampunk is post-apocalyptic fiction. In these stories, authors postulate that some kind of event, be it natural or human-made, causes society as we know it to crumble. Often, humans have exhausted the materials that power our world, such as petroleum. This creates a need for some kind of replacement. The heavy, durable materials of the past have a lot more staying power than the flimsy plastics we use today. This in turn leads to the human race falling back on earlier forms of technology, such as steam and clockwork, in the face of political or ecological disasters.

One good example of a post-apocalyptic setting with a steampunk feel is the world of *The City of Ember*. The tragedy that befell the earth is not elucidated until later installments of this four-part book series, and the time period is difficult to pinpoint. The citizens of Ember exist in a strange limbo between past and present, where they have access to electricity but have lost the knowledge of how or why the generator that powers the city functions.

You can also find this approach in *Terminal World* by Alistair Reynolds, which came out in 2010. In this scenario, the human race has been confined to a single city with different "zones" that support different levels of technology and includes a military comprised of airships.

The Mortal Engines series by Phillip Reeve takes a different approach. After something called "the 60 Minutes War," much of the world became uninhabitable. In order to survive, entire cities had to become mobile. In the first book of the series, we see the time of the "traction cities" coming to a close as prey (other towns) become scarcer and scarcer.

The Cinder Spires series by Jim Butcher also shows us a world that has become a harsh place. All of humanity is living in a series of giant towers far above the mysterious and terrifying ground. There are a few other changes, such as a race of enhanced humans called "warrior-born" and extremely intelligent cats.

On the other hand, there doesn't need to be some huge,

tragic event to facilitate people living with less technology far into the future. Firefly, for instance, is a wonderful space-western television series where the people inhabiting "the border planets" have much less access to technology than the central ones simply because of travel time. By expanding to new planets and moons, people find themselves living once again like pioneers of the old West with space ships instead of covered wagons.

Another good example of this approach is *The Iron Jackal* by Chris Wooding, where readers follow a crew of space pirates on their adventures. The massive territory and lawlessness of space creates perfect opportunities to draw parallels between the future and the past, even without any kind of disaster to precede it.

As you can see, making your Steampunk book, costume, or other kind of project feel "futuristic" can take a variety of forms. I've also seen some delightful mash-ups where people use the Steampunk aesthetic to interpret the droids of *Star Wars*, the Daleks of *Dr. Who*, and the Borg of *Star Trek*. Using tried and true futuristic worlds or tropes is another great avenue for making your Steampunk futuristic. So many Steampunk fans are also interested in other types of geekery, it's sure to get a smile from many of the people who see and recognize what you've done.

Chapter 14

For some people, Steampunk isn't Steampunk unless there is some connection to jolly ol' England. This appears to be more common within the wider European Steampunk scene. However, many of us find this view to be unreasonably limiting. The period surrounding the Industrial Revolution in the UK saw unprecedented opportunities for travel and exploration, and the people of western Europe became fascinated with (sometimes fictionalized) accounts of these journeys. These travelogues were influenced by the culture of the observers and can tell us just as much, or in some cases more, about the writers than the places they actually visit.

For instance, Jules Verne's contrasting characterizations of the phlegmatic Phileas Fogg (English), the emotional and adventurous Passepartout (French), and the short-tempered, violent Colonel Stamp Proctor (American) from *Around the World in 80 Days*, as well as the unflappable Hans (Icelandic) from *Journey to the Center of the Earth*, are all attributed to their country of origin.

He and Arthur Conan Doyle also capture classist attitudes that were prevalent at the time in *20,000 Leagues Under the Sea* and *The Lost World*, respectively. In both of these stories, there are the people who are really considered people (the aristocrats, scientists, and journalists) and those who are barely regarded as such (servants, fishermen, crew, and porters). For instance, in *20,000 Leagues*, Nemo gives the scientist his own room, and his servant and guide share one. When reading *The Lost World*, I was particularly struck by how at one point the narrator (journalist) laments being left "completely alone" by his comrades, when in fact there are several native people carrying his gear only a few feet away.

These attitudes were very real and abundant, and it is one reason that there are people who openly criticize Steampunk. They believe that to laud the writings and styles of those times is to celebrate this kind of bigotry and narrow view of the world. I completely disagree. Steampunk is a chance to confront issues like increasing wealth disparity and racism that still exist today.

We've made some great social strides in the last 100 years, but we are still far from having "fixed" these problems. Fiction is a wonderful way to open the discussion, not to mention the minds of readers. As authors, we can create any world we want, be it "true" to the times we want to reflect, or acting as a direct confrontation to the ideals of that period. Things can get a little trickier when it comes to costumes and other visual media simply because people have only a moment to see and interpret the intention behind something. (See below)

One of the best places to find information about multiculturalism in Steampunk is Diana Pho's "Beyond Victoriana" website. If you have never visited, I highly recommend it. This is the blurb from their homepage:

"Beyond Victoriana is the oldest-running blog about multicultural steampunk and retro-futurism – that is, steampunk outside of a Western-dominant, Eurocentric framework. Founded in 2009, *Beyond Victoriana* focuses on non-Western cultures, underrepresented minorities in Western histories (Asian / Pacific Islander, Middle Eastern, First Nation, Hispanic, black / African & other marginalized identities), and the cultural intersection between the West and the non-West."

I also enjoy the work that Suna Dasi and Yomi Ayeni do over at Steampunk India. The relationship between England and its various colonies during the Victorian era is a fascinating bit of history and cultural intersection.

There is, of course, much of the world that was never colonized by the Brits, and there were fascinating things going on during the time period most often involved in Steampunk. Bulgaria, for instance, has a very interesting history. While living there, I saw distinctive 19th century architecture from the neo-Byzantine period and learned about the turmoil and uprising against the Ottoman Empire during the 1870s. Somewhere down the line, I plan to use these events as a the basis of novel or series.

Another place I have called home is Greece, which faced impoverished conditions in the 1890s that forced many of its people to flee to the United States in hopes of finding a better life.

Spain had an Empire that rivaled England's and was in chaos after Napoleon's occupation (1808-1814), paving the way for multiple uprisings and changes of leadership. History is full of stories just begging to be told through a Steampunk lens!

The mid- to late-1800s also saw an unprecedented "opening" of Japan. Britain had colonies as far east as China, but Japan had remained totally isolated from the rest of the world until the American government negotiated the first trade agreement in 1851. By 1854, Japan was doing a brisk business in western Europe, and items like silk and kimonos were all the rage, and there are some beautiful examples of this in the Victoria and Albert Museum in London.

According to an article published in 1854, "In view of the events that have followed, the ending of Japan's self-isolation and opening of the country, first to American commerce and later to world-wise intercourse, must now be regarded as an achievement of momentous consequence, far exceeding in important all that even the most prophetic statesmanship of the time could foresee." (Matthew C. Perry)

And let's not forget that there was racial and cultural diversity within English-speaking countries. The experiences of free and enslaved Africans in the US in the period surrounding the American Civil War would have been very different than those of their white counterparts. Out West, it was largely Chinese immigrants who built the railroads, and the fight for the Alamo (1836) resulted in a victory for Mexico.

Bringing in some of this diversity can really add depth and interest to a story or costume, and you can be sure that many of the people living during the Victorian era would have been very aware of these goings on.

Do Your Research

At the same time, it is also important to integrate these different people and cultures in a respectful and, most importantly, well-researched way. Stereotypes are easy, truth is far more nuanced and takes more work. There are plenty of examples where the token person of color in a film is the villain and their entire characterization is from ridiculous stereotypes. This is not multiculturalism, this is racism.

A big part of writing any Steampunk novel set in some form of the real world should be doing ample research. There is nothing more galling to me than being presented with something that is out of time or place while reading. And yes, I am a Googler, and I will double check if something seems anachronistic in a bad way.

Of course, punking the status quo is an integral part of this genre, but much of the time, this is still historical fiction we're talking about. Therefore, any inconsistencies within the setting or people must stem from a conscious and deliberate change by the author that follow the internal logic of the world they are building. Otherwise, they run the risk of perpetuating harmful stereotypes through their own ignorance or bias, or in my case, sending me on constant trips to Wikipedia and ineffectual fist-shaking.

I want to give you a concrete example, but I also don't want to call too much negative attention to this particular work or author. So, let's just call her "X." In X's story, her protagonist travels to France, England, Italy, Austria, and Turkey. On the one hand, I applaud her for making England nothing more than a stopover and allowing these non-traditional Steampunk settings to shine. But on the other hand (which is the shaking fist), she made what appears to be a blatant error.

During some scenes in Constantinople, one of the characters hops in a rickshaw to get around the city. Though these human-powered taxis were popular in South and East Asian countries during the time period in question, an hour of searching could not find me a single historical reference to rickshaws appearing in Constantinople *ever*. If you've ever been confused about why the word "Oriental" is offensive, this is why.

You might just think I'm nit-picking, but think about it this way. In the West, rickshaws have come to be a symbol of the otherness of Asian peoples, something exotic for tourists to do if they visit India or China. If X's story were set in China, their presence wouldn't carry this connotation because they are historically accurate. But they have no business appearing in Turkey historically, so it seems the author must be trying to signal to the reader that they have entered a strange and alien land populated by "others."

This lumping together of all cultures East of the Balkans was not uncommon during the time period of the book, so if one of X's characters had said something erroneous about rickshaws, I would not have found it nearly as problematic. It would have been a way to show the person's level of knowledge about their own world. However, her characters are supposed to really *be* there in that time and place, seeing what there really was to see. As a reader, it felt as though the book fell back on a stereotype that is far from accurate.

I could also be wrong; perhaps X wanted there to be

rickshaws in Constantinople because of some other aspect of her world-building. (Though this seems doubtful given the overt changes that revolved around supernatural creatures and alchemy rather than anything geopolitical.) So, let's assume for a moment that this was a deliberate choice. If there was something about her world that made there be an infusion of East Asian culture in Turkey, then she should have let the reader know about it. There would have to have been some kind of huge political event to make that possible, and that would have been really interesting. If her story had been about an alternate history where China had gained control of Turkey then sure, go with rickshaws. But as it stands, they simply felt out of place and under-researched to me.

Costumes and props can also fall into this trap, but they have greater latitude than stories because they are more often based on an aesthetic rather than a narrative. Almost anything can be given a steamy makeover, be it *Battlestar Galactica*, home furnishings, or Sarah Palin. In this case, the colors and materials being used are far more important than situating a thing in place or time. However, this can become a minefield if a person outside of a culture or heritage decides they want to try another one on for size.

For instance, I have seen a rise in Indian-themed costumes lately, which pair a sari and traditional jewelry with awesome accessories like a brassy laser pistol and holster, and I hope to see more. Though if I, as a privileged white person, were to don the same ensemble, this could feel as if I am stealing this heritage. Even if in my own mind I am paying homage, this can still be viewed as an act of cultural appropriation. A good recent example of this is outcry against fashion designers for stealing patterns from Native Americans and African tribes, especially when they accidentally use something of cultural significance. A group of Romanian women flew to New York City during fashion week in 2018 to protest the appropriation of their embroidery motifs.

Some Steampunk-themed stories are set in the present but are based on an alternate history, and there are also some which are set in a post-apocalyptic future. In these cases, there is a bit more wiggle room when it comes to multiculturalism, but again, they need to be thought out fully and the internal logic must extend to all corners of the scenario. World-building grants the author the freedom to create whatever they choose, but they also carry the weight of making all of those choices.

So be mindful, be kind, and be informed when you want to integrate a culture other than your own.

Chapter 15

There is no denying the power of music. Even before babies can walk, if you put on music, they will begin to move their bodies to the beat. Rhythm is part of our species. Different eras have seen different instruments come and go, composers rise and fall based on the tide of opinion. For much of the history of Western music, this was tightly controlled by just a few people in high places. But just as popular literature came into its own during the steam era, so did popular entertainment.

In a previous chapter, I listed a few of the earliest Steampunk bands, many of which are still touring. The styles of music vary widely, ranging from Irish folk to goth rock to Souza's marches. There's room for moody jazz, "gypsy swing" (though this term is problematic with Romani people), bawdy cabaret, and lively drinking songs. One of the things I absolutely love about Steampunk music is that even more so than the costumes, props, and fiction, the musicians often have an infusion of other cultures in their final product. It's a big, beautiful mishmash of styles, instruments, and voices.

Some of these performers look more or less like any other kind of band, except that they wear Steampunk garb such as top hats and goggles during their performances. It's not uncommon to see elaborate face paint employed to give people an automaton feel. Other groups straddle the line between a band and a play. Each musician has a persona with a story, or as a group they recount tales of their daring antics as a crew of an airship. This flare for the dramatic is both in line with punk sensibilities, as well as harkening back to the steam era itself.

The Circus

Though the word "circus" dates back as far as Roman times, the only connection to the ancients is that is means "circle." This central feature of modern circuses developed from its roots in a different type of performance: the trick rider. These showmen would have their horses run in a circle as they did hand stands, jumped off and back on again, and performed other feats from the back of their steeds. Phillip Astley was one of these trick riders, as well as an instructor in horsemanship in London starting in 1768. He would teach in the morning and perform tricks in the evening inside of his 60-foot diameter ring, which he called his "circus." Astley was an unexpected success, but within a few years of starting to perform, audiences were hungry for more. He needed to bring in some other novelty acts to keep the audiences coming back.

Over the coming years, he sought many different types of performers. Jugglers, acrobats, and dancers helped to establish shows of strength and agility as part of the circus tradition, and they had music behind them to add drama to their performances. Another major contribution Astley made to what we now consider a quintessential aspect of the circus is that he brought in the clowns. Shakespeare had used the term clown to refer to his "fool" characters in some of his plays. In Elizabethan times, it came to be synonymous with a peasant or rustic simpleton, and later became a stock character to be opposite the sly "harlequin." Astley used these fools and their acts of slapstick to entertain his audience between acts. In the 19th century, the art of clowning became more sophisticated and expanded to include specific archetypes with different specialties and costumes.

In Europe, many large cities had permanent circus buildings. In the newly established United States of America, however, there weren't enough cities large enough to have this feature. In 1825, Joshua Purdy Brown created the first canvas circus tent to allow for moving his show around.

Whether stable or traveling, you can bet the circus had a band to accompany it. In Steampunk music, many groups call on the circus tradition to inform their songs. Though calliopes (steam-powered organs) are no longer common, electric keyboards can easily mimic their iconic hooting tones. Other times, their songs or personas are inspired by real or imagined circus acts. At a Steampunk convention, it is also common to see acrobats and contortionists perform to the music written and performed by Steampunk bands.

Burlesque and Cabaret

Contemporary burlesque usually involves a strip tease, but the artform that spread across the English-speaking world in the 1860s was far subtler. Yes, the female performers wore form-fitting outfits and tights, but that was about as far as it went. This was provocative in itself, and in later years the shows got steamier and steamier.

However, the most controversial aspect of early burlesque was the fact that all the parts were being played by women, and the troupes were often managed by women. They would take classic stories like Greek and Roman myths, then "punk" them by adding both music and social commentary. Usually, the music took the form of popular songs with altered lyrics, though sometimes original scores were written to support what was often referred to as "The Follies." This tongue-in-cheekiness is often just as important to contemporary burlesque as it was to its predecessor. And just like circus performers at Steampunk shows, burlesque performers also often draw from Steampunk music for their numbers.

A couple of decades after burlesque hit it big, cabaret emerged. It started out as a kind of "open mic night" for poets, but grew to include other types of spoken word, such as storytellers, and, you guessed it, musicians. This was especially popular in any establishment that served alcohol, as it gave patrons a reason to stick around and keep refilling their glasses. As the shows evolved, they often involved performers coming right out onto the floor and interacting with patrons. This type of floorshow continued to flourish right through the first World War.

Musical Theater

"Musicals" as we know them today are an offshoot of burlesque, cabaret, and later vaudeville. Unlike cabaret, they would be most often performed in theater with the audience distinctly separated, more like a ballet. In just the past couple of years, I've had the chance to enjoy several pieces of theater and dance that can be described as Steampunk. At the 2014 Edinburgh Fringe Festival, for instance, I got to see a Jekyll and Hyde ballet, a Dracula rock show using contemporary music, and a fantastic stage rendition of the Steampunk opera, *Dolls of New Albion*. I also attended two promenade musicals about Sweeney Todd and Dorian Grey, both of which involved the actors moving through the crowd as they performed and even dancing with us to make us part of the show.

Borrowing the Steampunk Aesthetic

In all of these cases, the music helped to draw in the crowd and heighten the feelings of the story. Musicians could be playing for laughs, for drama, or for tears, but they were definitely playing. With Steampunk's inherent flare and showman qualities, it's no surprise that we see so much music in the community. Performances by bands have become a cornerstone of Steampunk conventions, and many tour to different venues just like any other group of musicians.

However, the look and feel of Steampunk isn't limited only to bands that use that moniker. Other kinds of musicians have also jumped on the Steampunk bandwagon and borrowed the aesthetic for their performances. Here are a few examples of where you can find Steampunk cropping up in popular music videos and stage shows:

AC/DC - "Rock 'n' Roll Train" (video, stage production)
David Guetta feat. Nicki Minaj - "Turn Me On" (video)
John Hartford - Steam Powered Aereo-Takes (album)
Kurios - Cirque du Soleil (stage show)
Lovett - "Eye of the Storm" (video)
Mushroomhead - Qwerty (video)
Gary Numan - Splinter (Songs from a Broken Mind) (album)
Panic! At The Disco - "The Ballad of Mona Lisa" (video)
Rush - Clockwork Angels (album and Time Machine tour)
Smashing Pumpkins - "Tonight, Tonight" (video)
Lindsay Stirling - "Roundtable Rival" (video)
Tom Waits - Blood Money (album)
Therion - "Adulruna Rediviva" (video)

(Source: https://en.wikipedia.org/wiki/List_of_steampunk_works)

Chapter 16

MAKE IT PLAYABLE

For many, the joy of Steampunk is the ability to leave your everyday world behind. You can do this by attending conventions, reading fun and interesting stories, and watching awesome movies. And now more than ever, by playing a game. Whether you are looking for a computer game, table top role-playing game (RPG), or live action role play (LARP), the Steampunk-o-sphere has a game for you! And as the numbers of these games rises and the audience grows, there are chances for creators to get in on the action.

Adapting Something That Already Exists

Many of the stories that laid the groundwork for the Steampunk genre are old enough that they are in the public domain. The works of H.G. Wells, Jules Verne, and Sir Arthur Conan Doyle all fall into this category, and people who love these authors may be interested in playing a game. There are 56 different short stories and 4 novels about Sherlock Holmes, for instance, which could be adapted to a playable format. A person could add a technological twist or a supernatural element to the original plot lines to keep players on their toes, or plan a murder mystery dinner party based on a tale.

Alternatively, you could start with a game that already exists and add a Steampunk twist to it. For instance, a regular deck of playing cards with famous figures of the Victorian era or using gears and goggles rather than spades and hearts can add a steamy element to poker or cribbage. Bicycle_ brand offers a deck that adds metallic elements and gears to the existing suits, which proves there is an audience for it, so a creator could take this idea and add their own unique twist. There are a few different Steampunk tarot card decks, for instance. Cards Against Humanity is a hilarious game of filling in the blanks and playing the best (or most awful) thing you want, and you can get blank playing cards to allow players to add whatever they want to the mix, so why not add your own Steampunk elements? Personally, I am working on plans to make my own cribbage board either in a gear shape or using octopus tentacles as the tracks to add a little steam to my favorite game.

Dungeons and Dragons is a classic RPG, and with the right game master, there is no reason there couldn't be a Steampunk aspect added to it. Over at The Doberman Defense, Dr. X has written a great guide for the best ways to add blimps/dirigibles and robots to D&D. And if you are thinking about making your own RPG or LARP game, there are templates available so you don't have to devise your own scoring system. "D20" games are the most common (and complex) RPGs, and use 20-sided dice to decide how the action will proceed, but you can devise ways to use standard 8-sided dice for your own creation if you don't want people to have to get special equipment. There are also tons of miniatures (scale models of characters, creatures, and vehicles) readily available for people who want to add a visual aspect to their games. For many, painting these miniatures and adapting them to their own game universes is a big part of the fun of playing the game, but there are also pre-painted miniatures you can buy.

I haven't played any D20 games myself, but I LOVE strategy games like 7 Wonders and the Firefly tabletop game. These games use cards rather than dice and there is no game master who sets a unique task, but depending on the game there could be lots of different adventures to choose from. The character (or place in the case of 7 Wonders) dictates the kinds of actions you can take and what strategy you need to employ to succeed, so in that way it shares common ground with other tabletop RPGs. This notion could easily be adapted to a Steampunk setting, employing archetypes or real people from the Victorian era as characters.

Starting from Scratch

Do you have an idea for cool take on the Victorian era but you don't feel like you've got a novel in you? Consider making a game instead! If you like creating creatures and thinking about adventures that characters could have, but you don't want to try to fit it all into a single narrative, this could be a great way to get your creative vision out there without restricting yourself (or readers) to a single plot or set of characters. You lose a bit of the control, but it also allows your creation to grow and change in new and interesting ways.

Writing Your Own Interactive Murder Mystery Dinner

If you have attended a show like Tony N' Tina's Wedding or a murder mystery dinner theater, you may have already had your first LARPing experience without realizing it. These kinds of shows have a cast of actors, but they also require the audience to participate to some degree to work. Another related theater form is promenade, where the actors weave in and out of the audience (who is usually standing) and may interact with patrons on the sideline rather than directly engaging them in the plot. I went to a great example of this while I was in Edinburgh, and I thoroughly enjoyed being a part of the Victorian Vices pairing of *Sweeny Todd and the String of Pearls* and *The Picture of Dorian Gray*.

However, you don't have to go to a theater or special performance to get a chance to do some informal acting. A willing host or hostess can create a fun and unique dinner party in her own home by putting on a murder mystery dinner party. It may sound hard, but there are actually several websites and books out there to assist you either by providing kits or step by step guides for writing your own story. And the best part of creating your own mystery is that you can tailor it to any theme you want, including Steampunk.

I've got a few few tips compiled below, largely drawn from Hayley Games Productions, who offer a free download of

CHAPTER 16

a PDF entitled "How to Write and Host Your Own Large Group Murder Mystery Party." Here are some highlights from that document, along with my added tips for Steampunk specifically.

In a group of twenty, you will need 6-8 people who are in on the mystery from the beginning. They will need to play characters and interject important plot points at designated times to keep the game going. You don't necessarily need to write out a lot of dialog, bullet points with salient facts they must cover can be enough depending on the person. Smaller groups require a smaller number of allies.

Make sure you tell a story that goes beyond the murder itself. To make the game more fun for your guests, come up with an intriguing setting like the parlor of "the time traveler" from H. G. Wells' *The Time Machine*. Or you can create your own setting, like a cruise ship steaming across the Atlantic. Either way, make sure that the setting serves a framework on which to hang your characters and action. There needs to be a reason these people are all gathered together at that moment in time.

Every murder mystery requires a detective character, but they don't necessarily have to be a detective. This person needs to be able to take the reins and control the action and other characters and know the plot the best. When you are creating your other characters, make sure to throw in some red herrings. You need several viable suspects to make the game interesting, and it doesn't hurt if one of them also dies in the course of the investigation.

Most murders are motivated by love, revenge, or money, or some combination of the three. You don't have to rewrite the rules here, these are clear motives.

Don't let the game drag on for too long. Susan Haley-

Zemanak recommends keeping your mystery to only 90 minutes. She suggests this sequence of events:

Up to 15 minutes mingling and introduction where your "allies" set the scene for your guests.

Minute 15- Someone finds a clue that points to something shady about one of the suspects.

Minute 20- Find another clue, or make some physical action occur that brings another suspect into focus.

Minute 30- Big action that signals to the players the murder is soon to come. This can be a nasty fight between two of your characters, or someone drunkenly going on about a secret they know, for instance.

Minute 35- Kill someone. Leave an ambiguous clue at the scene of the crime.

Minute 40- After the body is removed, the detective character should take charge. Suspects accuse each other and reveal motives that have not yet been revealed.

Minutes 50-70- More clues or actions that establish the motive for taking out a second victim.

Minute 75- Second victim is discovered.

Minute 80- The detective sums up the various motives and evidence. Allow the audience to ask questions of your suspects and make guesses about whodunnit.

Minute 90- Wrap up the show. Make sure your killer confesses in a dramatic manner. They should get bodily removed from the scene, or perhaps try to take a hostage on their way out. The more action the better!

Joining the Table and Supporting Others

Not sure if the world of RPGs or LARPing is up your own creative alley? Try giving someone else's game a whirl. Conventions often host gaming as part of the festivities, so you could join a table and learn from other people's experience before setting off on your own. Or you could always ask your friends; you may be surprised to find out you already have access to some games through people you know.

Steampunk games also make regular appearances on crowdfunding platforms like Kickstarter and Indiegogo. If you make a donation you can often follow the creation of the game from start to finish and occasionally give input to the creators. If you aren't sure how to make your own game, supporting someone else can be a great way to learn about the process for yourself.

Chapter 17

MAKE IT SCARY

The world is a much safer place now than it ever was for our ancestors, and yet studies show that modern day people are extremely fearful. Despite the lack of wild beasties waiting to pounce, the taming of most diseases, and the relative comfort we enjoy, we are afraid. In a large part, this is due to the media and the way it over-reports tragedy in exchange for higher ratings. This is not a new phenomenon, but because of our unprecedented access to news sources on account of television and the Internet, the problem has continued to grow.

Likewise, it was not at all uncommon during the Steam era for newspapers and periodicals to do exactly the same thing to their readers. The general public could be whipped into a frenzy by a few carefully chosen words.

Jack the Ripper and Other Murderers

One famous example of this is the media hoopla over Jack the Ripper. This individual (or several people who copied one) is often referred to as the "world's first serial killer." Of course, this claim is doubtful, but it sure looked good in print. There are whole books devoted to trying to solve the case, making it far too large of a topic to cover in its entirety here. One of the most compelling things about the string of murders is that they were never solved, making it easy to come up with new interpretations. Here are just a few works dating from just after the murders (Aug-Sept 1888) to after Steampunk became a genre.

October 1888 - *The Curse Upon Mitre Square* by John Francis Brewer

1889 - "In Darkest London" by Margaret Harkness (under the pseudonym John Law)

1907 - In an early act of fan fiction, German publisher Verlagshaus für Volksliteratur und Kunst published "Wie Jack, der Aufschlitzer, gefasst wurde" (How Jack the Ripper Was Taken). Sherlock Holmes captures the Ripper in this one.

1911 - "The Lodger" by Marie Belloc Lowndes

1927 - Alfred Hitchcock adapts "The Lodger" as *The Lodger: A Story of the London Fog*. Four other adaptations followed.

1949 - *The Screaming Mimi* by Fredric Brown

1957 - *Terror Over London* by Gardner Fox

1989 - DC Comics releases "Gotham by Gaslight," the story of a steam age Batman on the hunt for Jack.

1992 - *Anno Dracula* by Kim Newman

This is a just a handful compared to the many works the fear and mystery surrounding the murders has conjured. Jack the Ripper's Wikipedia page has a full listing.

Jack may be the most famous, but did you know there were also other murders and serial killers who made their mark on the steam era? At the 2019 TeslaCon convention in Wisconsin, I had the opportunity to present a lecture called "Guilty by Gaslamp: Detectives and Criminals of the Steam Era." I looked at real life crimes, their coverage in the media, and how they captured the minds of notable authors. Here are a few examples.

The Tell-tale Heart by Edgar Allan Poe (1843)

This work is based on a real murder committed in 1830. The Knapp brothers hired a third party to murder Captain Joseph White after he changed his will to exclude a grand-niece who had married on of the Knapps. The case made plenty of headlines, especially because it was not a crime of passion, but involved a hired assassin. Some speculate that the loss of their case came in a large part because of the prosecutor, Daniel Webster. There are many parallels between The Tell-tale Heart and the courtroom discourse of Webster.

"The Bermondsey Horror" (1849)

Unlike the case that Poe drew from, this one did involve a body hidden under the floor. A husband and wife team, Marie and Frederick Manning, murdered her ex and put him under the stones in their kitchen floor. Frederick went to the victim's home afterward and stole money and railroad bonds. When friends of the victim reported to the police that the Manning house had been his destination that evening, they came to question them. Marie got spooked and stole the spoils of the crime from her husband and split. Frederick sold all of their belongings to finance his escape, which turned out to be in the opposite direction. Even so, they were both caught, mostly due to an important steam era invention: the telegraph. Though they had dissolved their victim using quicklime, the police were also able to make an identification using his false teeth.

When they were hanged, it was quite the spectacle. The crowd was so large and jolly, in fact, that Charles Dickens wrote a strongly worded editorial against the practice of public hangings. Wilkie Collins also made a passing reference to the Mannings in his 1860 release, *The Woman in White*.

Urban Legends

Jack the Ripper may have caught the popular imagination, but there were other stories that got blown up and disseminated by the media and word of mouth.

Spring-heeled Jack. He was first sighted in 1837 in London, and people claimed to have seen this strange figure for at least a decade to come. He supposedly attacked young women, breathed fire, and could leap over tall fences in a single bound.

Animals in the Sewers. Rumors of alligators in New York City's sewers still persist to this day, but did you know this wasn't the only city supposedly overrun with subterranean inhabitants? London was apparently infested with "The Black Sewer Swine of Hampstead." Rumors of these little piggies ensued for years and were even mentioned in an article in the Daily Telegraph in 1859. If given the choice, I am sure we'd all rather meet a pig in the sewer than a gator.

Visions of Crises. It was not uncommon for a person to report that they had received a vision of a tragedy as it occurred, even if they were in another part of the city. The newspapers would print their accounts of unaccountable panic and sightings of apparitions, and the public would eat it up.

Doppelgangers. What if there were someone out there who looked and sounded just like you, but were bent on your destruction? This was a real fear for 19th century Londoners, who would give accounts of chasing themselves through the streets or blaming their double for their own wrong-doing.

"New Humans." After Charles Darwin's treatise was released, many people began to believe in (and fear) the next step in human evolution. Some believed that humans and animals could be combined to make frightening creatures, such as the ones who populated *The Island of Doctor Moreau*.

Death by Garroting. In 1862, a man named Hugh Pilkington was strangled during a mugging. Soon, the story grew into a fervor as people feared a band of men roaming the streets and killing people at will.

Big Cats (or Dogs) Roaming the Countryside. Starting in

the middle of the 1800s, people began reporting sightings of large, black predators. Some described something like a black panther, while others reported seeing a huge black dog. The latter tales inspired the Sherlock Holmes novel The Hound of the Baskervilles.

As you can see, the supernatural only comes to play in a few of these examples. There were lots of things that people feared that were rooted in the mundane or in science (at least, science as they understood it then), and this made them susceptible to exaggeration by the media.

There were pranksters who played on these fears. With the help of the eager media and their willingness to disseminate them, the flames got fanned.

For instance, Mark Twain successfully hid a critique of utility companies in a story of murder and mayhem in 1863. A fiction by reporter Edmund Spencer about a man-eating tree in Madagascar circulated for years before it was revealed as a hoax. In 1874, residents of New York panicked as they read an account of zoo animals escaping and running rampant across the city, but the fine print at the bottom revealed it to be completely fabricated. The author, Thomas Connery, wrote the article to bring attention to the appalling conditions of zoo animals. If you are interested in reading about more hoaxes, you should check out the website for the Museum of Hoaxes.

There are many urban legends that I learned as a child or teen that are utterly false. For instance, "Daddy Longlegs" spiders are not extremely venomous, a tooth will not dissolve in a glass of Coke, and there is no man with a hook for a hand waiting to attack teenagers on date night. Yet, these stories persist. One can only conclude that humans like to be scared, disturbed, and titillated by these types of strange tales, and this was no different in the past.

Steampunk works can play on the fears that were actually reported, but there is ample space to create a new horror and support it by the same means as the Victorian-era pranksters. Rumor mills and the media spread fear better than any other means, and our capacity to believe these stories in the absence or proof, or even in the presence of proof to the contrary, is a testament to how much we delight in fright.

Something Real to Fear

I'm going to share with you my greatest fear. It's not ghosts or spiders, heights or public speaking. It isn't the call coming from inside the house or the zombie apocalypse. I have no problem with snakes, no stranger would brave the garbage heap of my back seat, and I get my best sleep during thunderstorms. I am afraid of something that is sometimes insidious and slow-moving or can strike without warning.

I fear madness.

Even though we have been studying the brain for centuries, there are still untold depths to plumb. Our realities are shaped by the chemicals, structures, and electrical currents going through our minds, and even a tiny imbalance can cause a person to tip toe over the edge. This has been on my mind a lot lately because I have been re-watching *Dollhouse*, where they stress that the "actives" (who have had their brains reprogrammed to be whoever the programmer makes them) experience everything as acutely and realistically as anyone else. They exist in a realm of total fantasy, yet they fall in love, suffer loss, and perform actions according to how their brains

CHAPTER 17

tell them to respond.

During the steam era, neuroscience wasn't even a word. Though some reforms in the treatment of the mentally ill occurred at the end of the 1700s, the rising tide of "undesirables" in later decades saw a return to poor conditions for patients. Insane people were shut away from the rest of society when they weren't put on display to be harassed by normal people. These mockeries of modern hospitals were the sites of abuse and even torture for the inmates, which was often carried out in the name of science. As much as I fear madness in my own lifetime, I wouldn't wish a Victorian-era asylum on anyone. "Lunatic asylums" are also a popular place for ghost hunters to visit due to the volume of tortured souls (and high mortality rate), making it a great setting for a horror story.

As scary as Dracula is, I have always been more creeped out by his bug-eating sidekick, Renfield. Sure, the Count will suck your blood, but at least he is consistent (not to mention polite). Renfield is by turns raving, endearing, violent, accommodating, and suicidal. It is one thing to be an undead monster, but to aspire to be an undead monster? That's messed up.

And clearly, it's not just contemporary people who thought so.

The Role of Madness in the Works of Edgar Allan Poe

(Many thanks to the lecturer from the Edgar Allan Poe Society at the 2016 Steampunk World's Fair who provided the basis for this section)

During the early to mid-1800s, mentalists had classified a few different types of madness, many of which correspond with conditions recognized by today's physicians. The practice of phrenology was also common, and involved the detailed study of the bumps on a person's skull to determine their personality traits. As a newspaper man and curious individual, Poe was clearly up on the scientific trends of his time. This included details in some of his best-known works that physicians of his day would have recognized.

"Bernice"

For instance, monomania appears as a central theme in a short story called "Berenice" published in 1835. This condition is characterized with an obsession over a single object or person. The main character, Egeus, is a man prone to fits of deep concentration. Even when his fiancée begins wasting away from some unnamed disease, he has trouble tearing himself away from counting shadows and other forms of obsession. Every part of her deteriorates, except for her perfect, pearly teeth, which becomes his newest focus. The story takes an even darker turn after she dies and he pulls all of her teeth to save as a keepsake. Too bad she wasn't really dead at the time…

"The System of Dr. Tarr and Mr. Feathers."

The narrator arrives at an asylum in order to study a new "system" of taking care of the mentally ill. He arrives too late in the day to meet any patients, but is invited to stay for dinner with the doctors and attendants. During the meal, his colleagues reveal stranger and stranger behavior. One acts like a chicken, while another suffers from the acute awareness that she was, in fact, a tea pot and not a lady at all. Meanwhile, the patients howl and carry on, and the medical staff shake their heads over the poor mad souls. Eventually, the narrator finds out that the inmates had taken over the asylum. It is actually the doctors in the cells. The very idea of what it means to be crazy and who decides is called into question by the power of context.

"The Fall of the House of Usher"

Poe's references to modern science were not limited to the plots of his stories, but found their way into character descriptions as well. In his infamous work, "The Fall of the House of Usher," Poe uses both a lengthy description and illustrations of the main character. Phrenology told people of that day it was possible to know that someone was generous or degenerate just by looking at their skulls and the shape of their eyes. And Poe incorporated these theories into his portrayal of the title character.

Madness as a Legal Defense

As the study of madness progressed, insanity became a plea that could be offered in court. Poe was especially interested in the notion of "temporary insanity" and the line between the sick and the well. As a reporter, he covered the murder trial in 1840 of a man named James Wood, who killed his daughter. Though the accused was found not guilty due to insanity, Poe clearly questions the verdict. In his coverage, he notes that the accused had a very calm, serene nature. The person who sold Wood the gun reported the same serenity while on the witness stand. This hardly sounded like the portrait of a manic man. Yet, his crimes were so heinous, the jury seemed to find it easier to believe he was insane rather than capable of such a terrible crime.

Two of Poe's most beloved stories are "The Black Cat" and "The Telltale Heart," and both revolve around a murderer who believes they have gotten away with their crimes. At least, until some sort of reminder or madness of their own drives them to reveal themselves. In both of these stories, Poe skirts the question of whether the narrators have always been mad, were driven mad and have now recovered, or descended into madness and never returned.

"Causes" and "Treatments" of Madness

Keep in mind, we are talking about an era where people thought bad smells caused disease, so the pathology of mental problems was not well understood. People on the margins of society, such as the old and female, were especially at risk of being labeled "insane." Many people believed that women had a smaller mental capacity than men to begin with because their skulls are generally a bit smaller, leaving less space for the brain.

For instance, women were thought to become "hysterical" because their wombs were wandering around their bodies.

CHAPTER 17

They could be driven mad by childbirth or by not giving birth. They could become crazy as a direct consequence of having a job (perish the thought!), or for having loose morals. One source I found said as many as 1/3 of mental patients were admitted due to nymphomania, or the "excessive excitement of the genitals."

Before the middle of the 19th century, mental illness was generally thought to stem from a sickness of the soul, not a physical ailment of the body. Mental health problems were akin to possession by a demon, and the people suffering from these ailments were treated no better than animals.

This changed in large part because of a bizarre event in 1848. Phineas Gage, an American railroad worker, miraculously survived when a railroad spike was driven all the way through his head. The injury destroyed much of his left frontal lobe, but he went on to live for another 12 years after the accident. But his friends would tell you that the Gage they knew didn't really survive at all. His whole demeanor and pattern of behavior changed due to the physical destruction of a specific part of his brain, and this discovery lead to a new theory of cognition.

As a result, the first recorded "psychosurgery" took place in Germany in 1888. Dr. Gottlieb Burckhardt performed surgery on six of his patients, only one of which showed any signs of improvement. The others saw no change, new symptoms, or died shortly after the procedure.

All those chemicals and structures I mentioned before were totally unknown to practitioners, but they did have a notion of the electrical activity in the brain. As early as the 1500s, people saw that some types of mental illness could be cured by "resetting" the brain through the chemical inducement of a seizure. By the 1800s, electroshock therapy was a fairly common treatment for a variety of mental conditions, many of which did not actually benefit from the treatment.

This was a time when it was okay to experiment freely on human patients, and as gruesome as it was, the research did lead to a better understanding of the role of electricity in the brain. In most cases, the strength of the current was not very high, and the patient was sedated during the treatment and did not suffer any pain as a result, but there was always someone somewhere pushing the envelope.

There were also different types of infections that could cause people to act insane. For instance, we now know that syphilis is a sexually transmitted disease caused by a bacterium, but the paralysis that can sometimes result from it were thought to be a separate mental disorder, and in the 1910s was treated by giving the patient malaria. Yes, you read right, they gave people malaria. Though fevers were attributed to aberrant behavior, some treatments of mental illness required the inducement of fever as the cure, which (unsurprisingly) could lead to more symptoms.

What Does This Have to do With Fear?

During much of the 19th century, being labeled as mentally ill was akin to a prison sentence. Inmates were chained to walls, physically restrained, drugged, beaten, and kept away from their families. It is no wonder that people worked so hard to conform to the dictates of Victorian-era society and were careful not to stray too far from the norm. Very few patients ever made it out of an asylum once they were admitted, and there was little regulation of what went on inside the walls. For a person living in the steam era, being "diagnosed" with any type of mental disorder due to their aberrant behavior would be a real and justifiable fear.

And unfortunately, the system is still broken, and marginalized people are still vulnerable. I remember reading a story lately about a black woman who was forcibly sedated and kept in a mental ward for days because she told an officer that Barack Obama followed her Twitter account. This successful, college-educated businesswoman was thought to be insane, though if anyone had checked they would have found that she was telling the truth.

For me, *One Flew Over the Cuckoo's Nest* is easily the scariest movie I have ever seen. There are no monsters, no blood or gore, none of the things that are traditionally at the center of a horror movie, but the notion of being trapped inside an asylum sends shivers up my spine. You don't need things that go bump in the night to create a tale of terror, human ignorance and the actions that spring from it are just as frightening.

Scary Steampunk and Foundation Works Recommendations

In the next chapter, I'll be focusing on supernatural Steampunk. This can be scary, but not necessarily. And what is scary for one person may not be a big deal for another. So, for the sake of these recommendations, I'm focusing on works that capitalize on the particular fears discussed in this chapter.

The Strange Case of Dr. Jekyll and Mr. Hyde, 1886, book by Robert Louis Stevenson

The Island of Doctor Moreau, 1896, book by H. G. Wells

From Hell, a Jack the Ripper movie, 2001

Dark Portals: Chronicles of Vidocq (or just Vidocq in French), movie, 2001

Devil in the White City, 2003, book by Erik Larson
Sweeney Todd, movie, 2007 (also various plays)
The Frankenstein Chronicles, 2016-present, television
Bodacious Creed, 2017, book by Jonathan Fesmire
The Alienist, 2018, television

Chapter 18

Steampunk isn't just about crazy technology and altering history, there is an undeniable supernatural element to many works as well, and for a very good reason. The Victorian era, as well as the period immediately before, saw a rise in belief in the supernatural. Why, in the face of technological advancement and rationalism, did this resurgence occur? And how can authors, makers, and gamers use this historical fact to their advantage?

Rational vs. Rationale

The Industrial Revolution saw the rise of many dichotomies that somehow managed to live side by side. Though it may seem strange to us at a time when we can get information on anything we want by poking a little box we carry in our pocket, during the 19th century, science itself was akin to magic. There were many advancements that worked, but people did not yet understand the how or why, only the results.

For instance, improving sanitation in a city could reduce the effects of cholera, and people believed that it was because plumbing cut down on bad smells rather than contagion by germs. Electricity brought light into their homes, but the average person couldn't tell you why that collection of glass and wires could outshine a candle. (And honestly, I would be hard-pressed to explain exactly how a telephone works myself!) In other words, people were willing to accept things that they could not explain.

Another factor of this era was a challenge to mainstream religious beliefs. Many felt that in Charles Darwin's 1859 treatise, *The Origin of the Species*, he had effectively killed God. By replacing God's will (and whim) with scientific principles and data, it shook the foundations of the major Western religions, which dictated that it was God alone who controlled the course of nature.

Charlotte Barrett put it this way, "The insertion of human beings into this biological continuum meant that, for Darwin, humans were part of nature rather than above it." Darwin was aware of how revolutionary his theories were, which is why he had originally planned to wait until after his death to publish them.

One might assume that this would be the perfect precursor to pave the way to a totally rational public, but people are far more complicated than that. Though many may have felt that the answers did not lie in words from the pulpit, there were still things that could not yet be explained by science. This left a gap between their experiences and their frameworks and opened their minds to alternative possibilities. The fantastical figures of myth held great appeal for people floundering in the face of religious and social upheaval.

Books Tell Us More than Stories

The literary audience of the steam era had a voracious appetite. The demand for serialized fiction and novels soared as literacy spread, and many jumped at the opportunity to meet this demand. Soon, publications were branching out in a variety of genres, some drawing from old superstitions and others creating new kinds of beasties.

Take Santa Claus, for instance. When Queen Victoria took the throne in 1837, there was no such thing as Santa, or even much popularity for the figure known as "Father Christmas." This figure comes from a midwinter festival in the English countryside and is a pagan character. He is tall, thin, and dressed in green as a symbol of the return of spring.

Saint Nicholas, on the other hand, is a Christian figure, but his purpose and abilities differ widely between sects. In Bulgarian Orthodox, for example, he's the patron saint of fishermen, and you celebrate his name day by enjoying a fish supper with your family. In Turkey, you definitely don't want to cross him because he kidnapped children and carried them off in a sack.

The mythic figure that most closely resembles Santa Claus is the Dutch "Sinter Klass." He's the one who is known to ride in a reindeer-powered sleigh and deliver gifts. His holiday falls around December 6.

In the strange and wonderful way these things have of developing, Sinter Klass didn't make the leap from Holland straight to Great Britain. Instead, Dutch settlers brought him over to the Americas, specifically to what would later become New York. According to Jona Lendering, Santa became an important symbol during the American War for Independence because he was specifically part of a non-English past. Many years later, British tourists returning from their travels abroad brought him home, and Santa Claus spread across Western Europe.

Only after a circuitous route, we finally end up with the chubby, jolly, red-suited toy man, as well as the morality he represents. Be kind and obedient little children, and you will be rewarded. Morality is an undercurrent in many stories of this era, regardless of what supernatural being it is who carries the message.

Fairy Tales

Compilations of "fairy stories" was one way to feed readers' fervor. Collections such as the Grimm Brother's *Children and Household Tales* were being read in nurseries throughout western Europe and eventually even farther afield. In addition to texts, this time period also saw an exodus as people moved away from the countryside to seek work in the cities. And they often brought their superstitions with them.

So, through both written and oral traditions, audiences of

all ages were being titillated by the strange creatures that inhabited the frightening forest, a place all too familiar to rural peasants but far less commonplace to an Industrialized society. Ironically, the reason for collecting these fantastical stories was often rooted in exposing the ignorance and backwardness of peasants. Yet once bound by the written word, they took hold of the imagination in a new way.

Though Industrialization may appear at first to be antithetical to belief in fairies, this antithesis itself was a driving factor in this particular belief's resurgence. London was not the only place where factories were built. In fact, factories began springing up all over the English countryside. Old maladies and new continued to persist, and some people blamed their problems on the factories driving away the fairies and their protection.

The use of fairy stories as morality tales also goes a long way toward explaining why they remained popular despite losing contact with their roots in the country. During my freshman year of college, my "Twice Told Tales" class spent half of a semester analyzing "Little Red Riding Hood." It turns out it isn't just a simple story of a little girl who gets lost in the woods, but serves a metaphor for womanhood, sexual transgressions, and the fear of strangers (i.e. immigrants). Stories were not (and are not) just a form of entertainment, but of indoctrination.

This and other tales also evolved over time, and different authors used its framework to promote their own agendas. For instance, in the original "Little Red Cap," she dies at the end. There is no heroic woodcutter, the wolf eats the grandma and the little girl up and lives happily ever after, ergo the fear of the dark stranger. Cinderella is propaganda geared towards women who want to better their lots in life (please the right man and all your dreams will come true). Rumpelstiltskin tells children to work hard or suffer the consequences. And you probably didn't know that the original Rapunzel ends up in her tower because her father was a thief.

Steampunk writers and filmmakers have also embraced fairy tales for inspiration. I already talked about both *Brothers Grimm* and *Hansel and Gretel: Witch Hunters films*, so here are a few recent books to check out.

The Queen of Clocks and Other Steampunk Tales, 2018 short fiction anthology (my horror retelling of Pinocchio is in this collection)

Gaslight & Grimm: Steampunk Faerie Tales, 2016 short fiction anthology

"Steampunk Red Riding Hood" series and "Steampunk Fairy Tale" series of novels by Melanie Karsak

Ghost Stories

Ghost stories appear in the folklore of countries all over the world. But ghosts as we think of them today in America and the UK where the majority of Steampunk stories occur have their roots in Spiritualism. Some people treated Spiritualism like a religion and others viewed it more as a science. Either way, it's based on the belief that spirits are hanging around waiting to have conversations with the living. And they do so by knocking on tables, moving around objects, and occasionally even taking a medium's clothes off. They speak through people who claim a supernatural ability or through the use of hypnotized

CHAPTER 18

volunteers. And very rarely say "wooooOOOOoooo!"

Most historians point to an event in New York in 1848—sisters Margaret and Katie Fox supposedly contacted a ghost and got media coverage—as the true beginning of the movement. Four years later, mediums started popping up in England and conducting séances. By the late Victorian period, many people claimed to have communicated with the dead.

Back in the United States, mediums especially found business booming after the Civil War ended in 1865. For a soldier to die in the field, rather than surrounded by his loved ones, was considered a "bad death." The fallen soldiers' relatives sought reassurances that their sons, brothers, and husbands were happy in the beyond.

In a time when class division and a clearly patriarchal society predominated, Spiritualism was a movement that crossed these boundaries. It could bring people from all walks of life into its fold. Women like Georgiana Eagle and Leslie Flint dominated the medium business during a time when most jobs were strictly for men. The 1860s saw a slew of pamphlets, newspapers, and public spectacles for the spiritually-inclined. They were read by prince and pauper alike.

Charles Dickens wrote one of the most famous ghost stories of all time: *A Christmas Carol.* Leading up to Victorian times, ghost stories were often told around the dwindling light of a fire during the holidays. But before the 1840s they were rarely written down.

Ruth Robbins, professor of English literature at Leeds Metropolitan University, attributes the popularity of ghost stories to the rise of periodicals. By the 1850s, these magazines had become hugely popular. Editors needed a massive amount of content to be competitive, so ghost stories began to be recorded en masse. *A Christmas Carol* was first published in this way in 1843, then compiled into a novel format later. Wilkie Collins, Elizabeth Gaskell, and Edgar Allan Poe, also found a platform for their ghostly stories in periodicals.

The thing that struck me the most while reading ghost stories of this era was how they actually weren't particularly scary. Usually, they were told by a first-person narrator. This eliminated the possibility that the protagonist would fall victim to a spirit. The facts are reported in a very straightforward manner and without trying to build suspense. Instead, they were often morality tales about the mistreatment of women and children. Or the guilty conscience of an old man (not unlike "A Christmas Carol" in that respect). So, if you are looking for a good scare, you probably won't find it in tales from the earlier end of their history.

Victorian households were the perfect setting for seances and ghost stories. Often, the homes of the aristocracy had been inhabited for generations. Plus, these old mansions and castles had creaking floorboards, unexplained drafts, and gaslights. We now know that leaks from these lights, as well as the CO_2 they emit while functioning properly, could cause hallucinations and the occasional fainting spell. Not to mention, their meager light did not reach all of the dark corners of a room. These homes often were equipped with "secret" passageways for servants to pass through unseen. So, there was a very real possibility of someone popping out at you with no notice, be it servant, medium, or "apparition."

Contacting the "beyond" was often conducted during private parlor sessions in one of these old houses. Besides talking to deceased loved ones, many of these sessions were specifically designed to contact famous people. Charles Dickens (who died in 1870) was one of the most popular spirits to contact. In addition to speaking through the mouths of mediums, ghosts would sometimes also use a typewriter or the like to pen a message from the beyond. Dickens died before he finished his last novel, and in 1873 an American author claimed to have been contacted by his spirit who dictated the ending of the story. Thus, the term "ghost writer" was born.

If you are interested in reading Victorian ghost stories straight from the source, I enjoyed the *Oxford Book of Victorian Ghost Stories* compiled in 2003. Here are a few other titles you might enjoy.

"Mrs. Zant and the Ghost," short story, 1885 by Wilkie Collins

No Rest for the Wicked, novel by Phoebe Darqueling

"The Eterna Files" series by Leanna Renee Hieber

The Spectral City novel by Leanna Renee Hieber

Ghosts by Gaslight, anthology

The Woman in Black, novel by Susan Hill 1983, play adapted 1989, and movie 2012

Crimson Peak, movie 2015

Vampire Stories

There are many different terms for vampires (also sometimes spelled vampyre in English), such as vyrkolakas (Greek), Bulgarian and Macedonian вампир (vampir), Bosnian lampir, Croatian vampir, Czech and Slovak upír, Polish wąpierz and (perhaps East Slavic-influenced) upiór, Ukrainian упир (upyr), Russian упырь (upyr), Belarusian упыр (upyr).

However, "nosferatu" was not actually a term in any language for vampire until it appeared in a 19th century travelogue. According to the accompanying essays by Michael Sims in the short story collection *Dracula's Guest: A Connoisseur's Guide to Victorian Vampires,* _ the word most likely came from a misattribution of a word that loosely means "devil" or "demon" in old Romanian. It actually referred specifically to the illegitimate offspring of illegitimate parents. Not exactly what we think of as vampires, so let's take a look at how we came to our current understanding.

Unlike today, it was not uncommon for people in the 18th-19th centuries to see dead bodies. This could occur directly after death or after they were dug up to make more room in over-crowded cemeteries. People treated public executions and other punishments, as well as dissections, like carnival attractions. Even though there was more exposure to the dead, the nature of decomposition was poorly understood. Sometimes corpses just refused to look the way people thought they would. It could be due to the amount of moisture or acid in the soil, the depth of burial, or some other factor. This led to supernatural explanations for totally natural phenomena.

The vampire as we know it in the English-speaking world is largely based on the same handful of European legends, and aspects of these stories have become canon. The Victorian era was the first time many of these stories were first recorded. This is what writers in the 1800s "knew" about vampires: They are dead (or, undead to be more precise); they are cold, on account of said dead-ness; they have bad breath; they drink blood. They do not necessarily drink blood in a malicious way, rather they are trying to prolong their existences. (Though of course, certain individuals, who were probably jerks in their regular lives, prove to enjoy mind games in addition to supper.)

As with ghost stories, the majority of vampire stories are told by a first-person narrator, but it is never the vampire. A survivor tells a tale to others, be it around the fire at Christmas or just to record it for posterity. This gives the stories the feeling of a warning or morality tale, again, not unlike ghost stories of this time.

Then there are the things that we all think we know about how vampires work, but only became established later. Films like Nosferatu (1922) and Dracula (1931) had a huge influence on modern perceptions of this monster. Both of these movies were both more or less based on Bram Stoker's 1897 novel. He added many details that we now think of as essential to "real" vampires (as opposed to *Twilight* and other variations that are maligned by vampire fans), but hadn't been part of previous tales in English. Here are some examples:

Vampires hate Christian stuff such as crucifixes and communion wafers. Despite being one of the first things a person will say if you ask them to describe a vampire, I didn't find many references to this particular phobia in my research. (Though prayer is a good way to keep some vampires away.) This appears to be a totally Victorian era addition to the lore. It may have had something to do with the belief that the bodies of heretics do not decompose.

Dracula could turn into other things, like bats, wolves, or mist. Not so for other vampires. They may have power over animals in older stories, but this seems to be more like a large predator scaring away smaller ones rather than some sort of magical ability.

They need to return to their coffins (or at least to the soil in which they were buried) in order to sustain themselves. Blood alone is not enough. Though many vampires rest in their coffins, before Dracula, this seems to have more to do with safety and secrecy than any real need.

Vampires hate garlic. This is from the Slavic vampire tradition, from which Stoker drew for his material. However, people in this part of the world believed that garlic was effective against a number of supernatural evils, including witches. If one was suspected of cavorting with the supernatural, they were given garlic either raw or cooked into a dish. This practice continued as late as the 1970s in some churches in the Slavic region, as well as stuffing the mouths of the deceased with garlic to keep evil spirits from inhabiting the body. But it was not necessarily strongly associated with vampires until Stoker and later works.

If you are interested in looking at the source material, I highly recommend Sims' book. The following is a list of vampire stories based on his selections, but there are certainly more out there. While many of these tales are old enough to be in the public domain, they can be hard to track down on their own.

A Mystery of the Campagna, Anne Crawford
A True Story of a Vampire, Eric, Count Stenbock
And the Creature Came in, Augustus Hare
Good Lady Ducayne, Mary Elizabeth Braddon
Let Loose, Mary Cholmondeley
The End of My Journey, George Gordon, Lord Byron
The Family of the Vourdalak, Aleksei Tolstoy
The Mysterious Stranger, Anonymous
The Tomb of Sarah, F. G. Loring
The Vampyre, John Polidori
Varney the Vampire, James Malcom Rymer
Wake Not the Dead, Theophile Gautier

As far as Steampunk goes, there are plenty of vampires to go around. (Disclaimer: I have not read all of these myself, so I can't speak to the quality.)

"Parasol Protectorate" series, Gail Carriger
"Scarlet Order" series, David Lee Summers
"London Steampunk" series, Bec McMaster
"Vampire Empire: series, Clay and Susan Griffith
"Immortal Empire" series, Kate Locke
Abraham Lincoln: Vampire Hunter, novel by Seth Grahame-Smith and movie
The Latitude of Temperance, novel, Ichabod Temperance
Anno Dracula, Kim Newman
Dracula, NBC television series
Penny Dreadful, television series
Van Helsing, movie

The Mummy's Curse

We all know the basic story. A tomb is opened, the archaeologists receive some kind of warning not the disturb the tomb. Later, a mummy rises from the dead to take his revenge. What may surprise you is that this notion is mostly a product of the Victorian era.

The ancient Egyptian culture and way of life is one of the longest lasting in all of human history. It spanned from the first people to settle in the Nile River Valley in 3500 BCE. Then, it fell to the Roman Empire with the death of Cleopatra VII (usually referred to simply as Cleopatra) in 30 BCE. Of course, this country underwent many changes during that long time period. There is still an Egyptian state today, but her death marked the end of active Pharaonic rulership over the territory.

Though ancient pharaohs sometimes left inscriptions warning off people from the desecration of their tombs, these were more than likely left for future pharaohs rather than archaeologists. It was common practice for a new pharaoh to remove the names from tombs of those who came before. They thought this promoted the notion a pharaoh was immutable. Only after modern interest in this ancient culture did the real idea of a "curse" come into being.

Scholars like Ailise Bulfin, in her article "The Fiction of Gothic Egypt and British Imperial Paranoia: The Curse of the Suez Canal" (2011), point to the conflict over this valuable real estate as the real cause the Mummy's Curse trope in literature. The Suez Canal is an artificial waterway created in 1869 and connects the Red Sea and the Mediterranean Sea. This allowed unprecedented access between Britain and its Eastern colonies. In due course, the so-called "Egyptian Question" became of vital political and economic importance during the Victorian era and beyond.

Many of the curse stories written during this time are aimed at satirizing the Imperial presence of Britain and its exploitation of Egypt.

By the late 1860s, several literary magazines were publishing Egyptian-themed stories and the notion of the curse of the mummy became more prevalent just as the Suez Canal reached completion. The very first story to explicitly mention a curse was called "The Lost Pyramids" and ran first in America and England in 1869, the same year the Canal was completed. In later reprints, they added the subtitle: The Mummy's Curse.

Here are a few Egyptocentric stories from the steam era if you want to consult source material:

The Mummy, A Tale of 22nd Century, Jane Webb

"Some Words with a Mummy," short satirical story, Edgar

Allan Poe

"The Mummy's Foot," short story, Theophile Gautier

"Lost in a Pyramid: The Mummy's Curse," short horror story, Louisa May Alcott

"The Ring of Thoth," short story, Sir Arthur Conan Doyle

"Lot 249," short story, Sir Arthur Conan Doyle

The Beetle, Richard Marsh

The Jewel of the Seven Stars, Bram Stoker

And on the Steampunk front, there are also great books and movies to choose from.

Nefertiti's Heart and *Hatshepsut's Collar,* "Artifact Hunter" series novels, A.W. Exley

Clockwork Cairo, short story collection edited by Matthew Bright

Changeless, Gail Carriger

The Clockwork Scarab, Colleen Gleason

The Extraordinary Adventures of Adèle Blanc-Sec, French film.

The Vocabulary

By a funny coincidence, when I first wrote the article that serves as the basis for this chapter, I was surrounded by books about the paranormal. My landlord was a statistician who crunches numbers for parapsychology studies, and I was using her office as my studio. When I would stare off into space to think, my eyes often came to rest on titles such as *The Medium, The Mystic and the Physicist; The Encyclopedia of the Paranormal,* and *Natural ESP.* People today often use terms like supernatural and paranormal interchangeably, but that isn't exactly correct. So, what is the difference?

"The realm of the paranormal includes things that we might one day understand, and be able to duplicate in a scientific study or setting and figure out just how they work– once we catch up to them. That includes things like faith healing, telepathy and telekinesis, and clairvoyance. There's also the field of cryptozoology: One day, Bigfoot might make the jump from paranormal to fact, much like the giant panda, the giant squid, the giraffe, and the okapi once did.

Supernatural things, on the other hand, we will never have a way to document simply because they don't play by the same rules we do. We'll never have a way to scientifically observe a god, a guardian angel, or a soul. We're not going to be able to repeat a miracle in a laboratory. The supernatural is beyond our capabilities of understanding and is instead in the realm of the divine or otherworldly."

(Source: https://knowledgenuts.com/2014/02/20/difference-between-paranormal-and-supernatural)

It seems pretty clear laid out like that. But in the 19th and early 20th centuries, there were a lot of people trying to bring supernatural things into the realm of scientific explanation (the paranormal). So, it's not surprising that there is conflict about the terminology and its correct application even today.

To confuse matters, there is also theosophy, or the science of the occult. This is a subject fit for its own article at some point in the future, but in brief, theosophy in the 19th century was a movement that promoted the elevation of the human being through a deep connection to the Divine (which may be called Nature). It was basically the idea that people could evolve into higher beings through their study of and tapping into some higher power. This could be the god of the Judeo-Christian-

Muslim heritage or some other divine entity. It simultaneously embraced the idea of evolution while also rejecting the idea that god no longer had a role to play.

But for now, let's concentrate on the interplay between supernatural and paranormal, and the means of converting the unknowable into the knowable.

Looking for Proof

Not everyone was taken in by just the stories, they wanted proof of the supernatural. And as that master of the fantastic, J. R. R. Tolkien tells us, "There is nothing like looking, if you want to find something. You certainly usually find something, if you look, but it is not always quite the something you were after."

Of course, believing isn't everything. In fact, seeing isn't always believing either. In the face of the rising claims of communications with ghosts and sightings of storybook creatures, people often turned to hard science. Or at least as hard a science as they could manage in a time when bloodletting was still a common cure for various illnesses. And just as quickly, people found ways to substantiate their claims even if they were completely false.

Capturing an Image

The word "photography," which roughly means "light-writing," was coined in 1839 by chemist and inventor Sir John Herschel. There were some cameras prior to this year, like the camera obscura, but 1839 saw the birth of many photographic techniques that were employed throughout the century. In this same year, Louis Daguerre introduced the "daguerrotype" method of photography, which did not require the hours of exposure necessary for a camera obscura. It can be hard to get those pesky pixies to stay still for long, so these advancements made it possible for the first time to claim photographic proof, and so objective "scientific" proof, of the supernatural.

Within a few decades of photography's commercial success, "spirit photographers" emerged. They took photos during seances and documented the presence of ghosts, as well as the ectoplasm the mediums often exuded during spiritual encounters. Mediums would pull this spirit goo (which bore a striking resemblance to cheese cloth) out of all kinds of orifices (and I do mean all) to show a physical manifestation of contact with the beyond. The "ghosts" were sometimes mannequins the mediums worked with a pulley, or were created by the photographer during development.

Though they may not have had Photoshop in the steam era, they certainly had trick photography. It didn't take long for people to realize that they could alter negatives and combine multiple photographs to create false images that looked totally real. Headless portraiture was all the rage, and simple to do by cutting and piecing together a negative.

Holding it in Your Hand

One big difference between tales of encounters with ghosts and the experience of a séance was the presence of ectoplasm. (Think Slimer from Ghostbuster.) False mediums claimed this substance was behind floating tables and other parlor tricks, as well as occasionally being excreted by them while in a trance state. Some also claimed that this was also the means for spirits to take a visible form. So, the "ghosts" that would appear during a session would be draped with sheets or strips of gauzy fabric or cheese cloth.

Ghost stories, on the other hand, make no mention of ectoplasm. The most famous ecto-hoaxstress was an Irish medium named Kathleen Goligher. Her sham did manage to fool at least one engineer-turned-psychical researcher, William Jackson Crawford. But the sketchy photographs of ectoplasm (which often "emanated" from Goligher's genitals) and the closed-door nature of their sessions did little to convince the rest of the growing community of researchers that her claims were true.

Measuring the Unknown

Karl von Reichenbach made his name as a chemist and industrialist. He discovered paraffin, creosote, and indigo dye, just to name a few of his achievements. He also collected meteorites and wrote treatises on them at the time when most academics thought the idea of stones falling the sky was pure fantasy. Rather than simply ride off into the sunset with his vast wealth, von Reichenbach turned his sights on a mysterious malady: sleepwalking.

He conducted a massive survey among the villages around the Danube where he had his holdings and found that not only was "somnambulism" fairly common, but people also suffered from other nighttime maladies like night terrors and spasms. Futhermore, they appeared to occur on a regular cycle that followed the natural rhythms of the moon.

Over time, he determined that there were people who were more sensitive to an invisible force exerted by both the sun and the moon. When he first began exploring the idea of an external cause, he looked to some variation of electrical energy as an irritant. He turned his focus to natural phenomena such as lightning that could possibly trigger a reaction in those who suffered from the maladies, most of whom were children. However, he never found the connection to electricity he was looking for.

Instead, he hypothesized a different force at work. He gave it the name "Odic force" for the god Odin because he saw it as a pervasive wave phenomenon that coursed through all things, living or inanimate. Von Reichenbach was the first to coin the term "sensitive" to refer to people with extra-sensory perception, though most often we now see that term applied to mediums.

His studies and experiments eventually led him to believe that sleepwalkers were sensitives who suffered from a natural lack of the type of Odic force put off by the moon. They craved it and acted on those cravings by getting out of bed and going out in search of the right kind of light. People who suffered from cramping and terror as the sun went down had a similar affliction, only they craved sunlight. The loss of those particular waves caused them pain until the sun returned.

As his studies progressed, he identified the most sensitive people among his charges and started to conduct experiments inside of completely dark rooms. He had access to all kinds of materials, both geological and humanmade. Once the sensitives had become acclimatized to the full darkness, one of these substances would be introduced to the space using a trap door, and the sensitives claimed to see colors and lights coming off of them. He also ran wires into the room that were attached to metal plates that collected either sunlight or moonlight. The sensitives would stay in the complete darkness long enough that they could not know whether it was night or day, but still consistently reported that moonlight caused irritation akin to heat. Sunlight produced a soothing coolness. Von Reichenbach theorized that Odic force was not light itself, but something carried on light waves.

He applied the same scientific rigor to these studies as his work in chemistry, which is of course somewhat relative given he was working in the 1800s. Many scholars both during his time and ours believe he suffered from confirmation bias, and his studies never made it very far into mainstream.

His work is sometimes lumped together with that of Franz Mesmer and his 18th century theory of animal magnetism. Von Reichenbach addresses mesmerism in his own book, *Odic-magnetic Letters,* published in 1860. You can read the full text (translated from German) online. It's fascinating stuff that applies his theory of Odic energy to bells, fermentation, decomposition, water-finding, and a variety of other processes and practices.

Chapter 19

Do you remember the first time you had a crush? Well, how about an author-crush? That's what I call it when I find an author whose work I enjoy so much that I feel compelled to read his or her entire collected works. In recent years, this has included Arthur Conan Doyle and Jules Verne, but it all started with Kurt Vonnegut. I vividly remember the experience of reading *Slaughterhouse 5* in high school, and within a year I had read every one of his 14 novels. Not only was *Slaughterhouse 5* a gateway to science fiction in general and Vonnegut specifically, but it was my first exposure to time travel in literature.

In Vonnegut's story, the main character, Billy Pilgrim, is "unstuck in time." He does not travel to the faraway past nor the distant future. Instead, he is able to travel along his own timeline, from birth to death, and is doomed to do so forever. For the reader, the story takes one through different events in his life, but not in a linear fashion, and he always returns to the same experience. He and his platoon were trapped in a slaughterhouse during the bombing of Dresden in WWII (like Vonnegut himself), and he finds himself reliving this trauma over and over again. Pilgrim makes these journeys within his own body, he is not watching the events of his life unfold from outside himself. Rather, he re-visits scenes from his life, but is powerless to change them.

When a person mentions time travel, this is not what usually comes to mind. Generally, we think of a person climbing into a contraption such as the one in H. G. Wells' classic, *The Time Machine,* and riding their way through time, their own body unchanged. This may happen purely out of curiosity, but as often as not the goal is to avert a disaster. In some earlier chapters, I already addressed alternative history and adding futuristic elements, so it might seem like there isn't anything left to say about time. I may have discussed the past and the future, but that still leaves us with the mechanics of time travel.

I received an incredible collection of short stories called *The Time Traveler's Almanac* as a birthday gift a few years ago. This tome, numbering a whopping 948 pages, was edited by Ann and Jeff Vandermeer (of *The Steampunk Bible* fame), and contains the best of the best when it comes to time travel fiction. In addition to tales written by notables such as Ursula

K. Le Guin, William Gibson, Ray Bradbury, and Isaac Asimov, there are very interesting essays that divide the sections. The information in this article is largely adapted from "Time Travel in Theory and Practice" by Stan Love.

Moving Forward

We are all traveling through time, it is simply in one direction at a uniform speed of 3600 seconds per hour. This doesn't sound nearly as fun as it is to imagine a quick jaunt to the Jurassic or popping over to 2300 for a cup of hydroponic super coffee. This is the stuff the imagination, of science fiction. But hard science does offer some interesting tidbits about what we could expect from time travel with the knowledge we already have.

Albert Einstein offers us two theories concerning traveling forward through time, a General one and a Special one. General Relativity has to do with the interaction between extremely massive objects and smaller ones that are trying to escape their gravitational pull. Now, assuming that your ship can move at just barely slower than the speed of light, and you are trying to get away from, say, a black hole or a neutron star, time acts really funny. Inside the ship, time will slow down, at least as it appears to an outside observer. If you get too close, the tidal forces of the black hole will tear you apart. The side of the ship facing the gravitational force would experience a stronger pull than the other side, and stretch away from the other side of the ship, causing the whole thing to elongate. This phenomenon has the delightful name of "spaghettification" or "the noodle effect." The side closer to the gravitational force will also experience time slightly differently (due to gravitational time dilation) than the side that is farther away, and both of these are different than what the outside observer experiences.

When I learned about Special Relativity, I was in a delightful class with the nickname of "Physics for Poets" (the more lyrical counterpart to "Rocks for Jocks"). My professor was a long-since tenured, adorable old man who wrote and illustrated his own text book, which meant stick figures and rudimentary rockets. He explained the classic Twin Paradox of special relativity using stick figures named Moe and Joe (and later their sister Roe, but we only need the first two for this theory). This thought experiment has been part of the discussion of physics since the early 1900s and will remain a thought experiment until we are able to travel at near light-speed.

All right, so there are twins named Moe and Joe. Moe gets into a rocket ship, and Joe stays behind on Earth. As Moe's rocket approaches near light-speed, Joe checks in with a telescope. Moe will appear to be moving in slow motion from Joe's outside vantage point. Moe's clock will tick at a slower rate than Joe's, and the wavelengths of the light source in her rocket will shift toward the red end of the spectrum (because they are being made longer through the noodle effect). When Moe returns to Earth, she will have experienced a fraction of the Earth-time that Joe did, and so Joe will be older. There is a lot of math and experimentation with super small objects to back this up, and you are welcome to explore that further on your own if you are really into facts and figures, but the stick figures and kindly old professor was good enough for me.

So, in theory it is totally possible to move quickly into the future, but so far we haven't come even close to reaching the speed required to try it out with a human being. A person would have to get up to about 300,000 km/second in order to do this, and so far we have not discovered an energy source capable of generating this much energy. And frankly, if we did, I doubt we would use it to hurtle someone into the future. Because, like I said, we are already moving into the future all the time.

Backing Up

Hindsight being 20/20 and all, I am sure there has been some time in your life when you wished your older and wiser self could travel back in time and warn your younger self to avoid a mistake or just to give encouragement that things will eventually look up. As grown-ups, we know that the drama of high school quickly falls away after graduation, and that college life undergoes the same treatment within a few years of moving into the working world. But, in our limited conception of time, we are always going to see what is in front of us as the sharpest, strongest, most important thing that is happening and will happen.

In the aforementioned essays by Stan Love, he tells his readers that he learned most of what he knows about traveling backward in time from Kip Thorne, so if you want all the details, check out Thorne's book, *Black Holes and Time Warps: Einstein's Outrageous Legacy.*

There are actually several theoretical methods for creating a time machine, there just haven't been any ways to test them. And there likely won't be any ways to test them for hundreds, if not thousands of years. But waiting is no fun, and a good imagination is a great replacement for hard facts, so let's move on to the theories. Now, bear with me, I am not a physicist nor a mathematician, but this is all weird and wonderful food for thought.

CHAPTER 19

One theory involves an infinitely long cylinder. We are not just talking about the width of the known universe here, this would be infinity. Apparently, physics allows that if this cylinder existed, and was turning at nearly the speed of light, then vehicles moving through it would be able to make specific flight paths to the location they left, but at an earlier time. The best part? We may not even have to build this infinite cylinder ourselves. There is room within our current understanding of physics for a naturally occurring structure with these properties to already exist. It is a "linear black hole," also known as a cosmic string.

This is not to be confused with a wormhole, which would be a tunnel created by the connection of two black holes. In general, this theoretical mode of travel (also known as an Einstein-Rosen bridge) is most often associated with moving faster than light speed over great distances, and it is also related to time travel. In General Relativity, Einstein shows that space and time are two aspects of the same thing. You cannot mess with one without influencing the other. So, an astronaut traveling through a wormhole that is essentially warping space will also experience a shift in time as well. If one could manipulate the wormhole to pick you up and spit you out relatively close in space (think like a big C shape with the earth being embraced by the arms), then you return to Earth, you could theoretically travel back (or forward) in time. The catch? You can't ever travel back farther in time that when the wormhole was established, because you need an end to come out of. People living far enough into the future could take a jaunt back to meet their great-great-greats.

All right, so we have a couple theories that involve black holes, which do exist. But there is that whole spaghettification problem. Black holes are made of incredibly destructive forces that pull things apart atom by atom, so even if a wormhole existed and we could make it point where we wanted, how would we survive the trip? Black holes are extremely unstable, and any tunnel created by joining two of them would be likely to collapse at any moment. We would need to use something that is emptier than a vacuum and lighter than nothing to counteract the effects of the gravity well. Sound impossible? Nope.

Through something called the Casimir effect, it is actually possible to create negative pressure. There is a long explanation that has to do with making photons do weird things between materials that are poor conductors, but just take my word for it. If one were to construct two spheres, one inside of the other, out of these poorly conducting materials, and trap photons between the two layers, the photons outside the spheres would cause this negative pressure to occur. Granted, it has only been measured in extremely tiny increments, but *it has been measured*.

As I said, hard science can really only take us so far. The implications and intellectual appeal of time travel has very little to do with physics in the end. Now that we got all of that boring science and "reality" out of the way, it is time to move onto the fun parts of time travel. Before we can explore the repercussions of time travel, however, we have to take a look at our understanding of time itself. Namely, is there a single timeline or infinite possibilities? (This is of course assuming that time is linear at all, but that is a much bigger discussion for another… time.)

CHAPTER 19

There Can Be Only One

So, let's say there is just one timeline. One classic example of the danger here is called The Grandfather Paradox. A time traveler goes back in time and accidentally kills his own ancestor, thus ending the family line. He can't return to his present, because he will no longer exist. The only way for him to ensure that the family line continues is to impregnate his grandmother, thus becoming his own grandfather.

Personally, I find this particular thought experiment a bit silly considering that we know how DNA and the transference of genetic material works. If the time traveler did, in fact, kill his grandfather, impregnating his grandmother would not result in an exact copy of himself two generations later. Conversely, if killing his grandfather were to cause him to never be born, then he would cease to exist the same moment that his grandfather's heart stopped beating and wouldn't have time to woo his nana (ewww). If he did not immediately blink out of existence, I suppose that grandpappy might have had some of his little swimmers on ice, but that would really be the only way around it.

However, here is the thing about linear time. In a universe with only a single time line, every decision that is ever made, has ever been made, will ever be made, is already certain. That may seem like a bit of a leap, but think about it this way. Your present is someone else's past (let's call her Amber), and someone else's future (who will be known as Zoe). To Amber, the time at which you are reading this sentence is the future, which seems uncertain and full of possibilities. From Zoe's perspective, however, the events of the past are set in stone, immutable and measurable.

The "truth" of these events could be obscured, but the events themselves happened the way that they happened. And Zoe's present is someone else's past, and so on, and so on. In this case, the act of time traveling is moving up or down along this single line, and the actions that take place there have happened, are happening, and did happen already.

Some authors and movie makers get this right. In *Harry Potter and the Prisoner of Azkaban*, for instance, Harry and Hermione end up going back in time a few hours to save Harry's godfather. During the first time through these three hours, a few mysterious things happen. Rocks fly through Hagrid's window, alerting the teen wizards of the Minister's approach. Later, a howl in the distance distracts the werewolf that is attacking them, thus leading it out into the forest and saving the kids. When Harry and Hermione go back and revisit these events, Hermione realizes that it must've been she who threw the rocks and made the howling sound. She acts because she knows that she has *already* acted.

Another series that does a lot with teleportation and time travel and handles it brilliantly are the "Dragonriders of Pern" series of books by mother and son team, Ann and Todd McCaffrey. If you have never read these books and are looking for a world that straddles fantasy and science fiction to fall into, I highly recommend them.

To Infinity, and Beyond!

The other side of this cosmic coin is the idea that there is one timeline for every choice made by every person who has ever lived because reality splits based on these untraveled roads. There is a world where you had strawberry jam on your toast this morning, and another where you had grape jelly. If that sounds daunting, keep this in mind: people are not special. If we follow this idea to its logical extension then there has to be a new branch of existence for decisions made by the human race, then there must one for every dog, fish, amoeba, and atom that makes up the known (and unknown) universe.

Let's bring our time traveler into this scenario. He travels back in time, or he doesn't. He makes it to the right time, or he doesn't. He eats a cheese sandwich, or he doesn't. While choking on the cheese sandwich he steps on a man's foot, or he doesn't. This man is his grandfather, or he isn't. The maybe grandfather man is angry, or he isn't. They draw pistols at dawn, or they don't. The time traveler kills his grandfather, or he doesn't. Not to mention what anyone decides to wear that day, whether they put on aftershave, kissed their kids goodbye, or put on their pants starting with the left or the right.

For the sake of stories, people don't generally roll with this notion to the extent that I just demonstrated, because it gets confusing and weird and bogged down in details about pants. Some people only focus on life-changing events or big decisions, such as where to go to college or missing the train where you would have met the love of your life. They figure the stuff about pants will probably work itself out and amounts to very little in the grand scheme of things, and they are probably right. It mattered very little what I was wearing or what I had for breakfast the day that my husband's eyes met mine across the crowded lecture hall, but the fact that I signed up for a class so far outside my major made all the difference.

Let us return to our time traveler. We can't totally abandon everything in the multi-verse, because some choices *do* make a big impact. In the case of the traveler, the fact that he traveled through time at all is a huge deal. It seems safe to assume that ripping the fabric of space and time asunder would be enough to create a new branch of the time line. Next, killing Grandpa (let's call him Mr. Smith) would definitely count as a big deal, at which point time would bifurcate again. All right, so in this one branch of time where the traveler went into the past, Mr. Smith is dead. But this is still linear time we are talking about here, and the split between time travel and no time travel occurred *after* the events in Mr. Smith's day, so the time traveler would be safe from disappearing. Instead, there would be a whole new branch of time that snapped into existence to reflect the absence of Mr. Smith.

So, the time traveler will not blink out of existence. In fact, even if he went back to when the most advanced creature on the planet was a reptile and killed them all, he would still exist in the multi-verse. The biggest issue, then, becomes picking out the right timeline to land in after the trip is over.

Back to the Present

Please do not mistake these ruminations for lack of love or respect for time travel tales. I enjoy them precisely because they make me think about things like this. The idea of visiting another time line where the choices were all different is an exciting train of thought, and exploring these meanderings through time in stories is a unique way to navigate an examination of the human condition. In a way, traveling into the distant future is a way to cheat death. Traveling into the past allows an opportunity to see our roots and find out more about what brought us here in the first place. We experience the present so clearly, looking for a way to bring the past or future into such focus is not just understandable, but laudable.

I gave you a couple examples of non-Steampunk works that deal with time travel, so here are a few Steampunk

CHAPTER 19

recommendations.
- "Burton and Swinburne" series, Mark Hodder
- "Nomad of the Time Stream" series, Michael Moorcock
- "Keeping Time" series, Heather Albano
- *Morlock Night*, K.W. Jeter
- *Anubis Gates*, Tim Powers

Chapter 20

MAKE IT YOURS

I don't usually court controversy.

I do my best to stay out of the debates over whether or not something is "really" Steampunk because all they do is make me angry. Instead, I prefer to look at the things people have called Steampunk and then highlight what I see that is consistent with any aspect of the genre. Perhaps it is my background in Anthropology that makes it so, but my approach is usually descriptive, not proscriptive.

In other words, I see myself as a participant-observer

looking for patterns and meaning without trying to define the boundaries. And I recognize the irony of having a chapter that's a bit of a rant about what it means to really embrace Steampunk while criticizing people who go on rants about what Steampunk means... but here goes.

Being part of a fandom (or in anthro-speak, a "microculture") shouldn't hinge on limiting other people. The point isn't to tell other fans they can't participate, like an entire genre/aesthetic/cultural tapestry is a ball you aren't willing to share just because someone wishes to participate on their own terms, because their vision of what is to come is different than what has come before. Or maybe the creator does not have the funds or technical skills to execute what their imagination has produced, and that creative impulse should not be snuffed out.

Here's an Example

I saw a quote by Evelyn Kriete, one of the creators of *The Steampunk Bible*, made into a meme that said:

"Every time someone says something isn't Steampunk, a kitten is eaten by a dragon. Do you really want to be that person that leads to kittens being eaten by dragons?"

I loved the sentiment and reposted the meme immediately. However, this was not everyone's reaction in the Facebook comment thread where I originally found it.

Many of the people who responded made jokes, such as "But what if I like dragons better?" and "Dragons have to eat too!" A few people supported the statement. But it seemed to me as I watched the comments accumulate that most people *completely* missed the point. They responded along the lines of "But if something ISN'T really Steampunk then I should be able to say so" and "Sometimes people are just wrong and they need to be put in their place."

This one got the most thumbs up, and manages to miss the point twice by both making a joke about dragons and by being ignorant:

"If it's not Steampunk, then it's not steampunk... If a kitten dies everytime [sic] I say a cactus is not steampunk just because you glued some gears on it (a very bad example, but you get my point) so be it. I've always rooted for Khaleesi and her dragons anyway."

This response couldn't be more wrong.

Let me Break it Down

If the person who made the gear-cactus was inspired by classic sci-fi literature or anything at all in the Steampunk canon, then the thing they create *is* Steampunk because it was influenced *by* Steampunk or its roots. It is *that person's* contribution to the ever-evolving discussion.

You don't have to like it. You're welcome to think that it is not as high quality of an item as an actually fully clockwork cactus would be. You can believe that it isn't the best example of Steampunk. But that doesn't mean it *isn't* Steampunk.

Second, if a person has a vision of a clockwork cactus but they do not have the money or skills to make exactly what they imagine, does that mean they should not be "allowed" to create at all? Imagine you are that gear-gluer and you finally get up the courage to post your creation because Steampunk is all about DIY, right? The Wild West is a popular backdrop for Steampunk and in the story you are writing there is a whole battalion of clockwork cacti poised to attack a backwater town.

And then when you post your vision of a clockwork cactus you are met with a tide of criticism telling you that you failed to create something Steampunk and people are not interested in your contribution. They are effectively telling the creator to shut up and sit down.

And this is an act of violence.

Not only is it an act of violence, it completely undermines punk, and so Steampunk, as an ethos. I know how us geeks like to be technically correct (which is the best form of correct) but there needs to be room for kindness and encouragement as well. Why police the way people interact with the things you both love when it's so easy to find common ground instead?

The person who says the gear-cactus isn't Steampunk could just as easily say: "It would be so cool to see this a as a fully functioning clockwork machine!" That would acknowledge the effort and vision of the creator and allow the commentator a chance to express themselves, but no harm is done.

Steampunk (and Fandoms) as Identity-Building

In the act of building our identities, our contained sense of self, humans find it easiest to split the world into a series of opposites. As a species, we are prone to pattern recognition, and then we use the patterns to shape who we are and how we interact with the world. Dichotomies are simple and easy to understand. The act of trying to define Steampunk can be an act of identity-building for those engaging in the conversation.

It's a valid process that applies to fandoms across the board. It is true in all genres; people everywhere nitpick details of the things they love. However, just because the propensity is there, it doesn't mean that it is the most productive way to look at the world.

I believe a lot of the backlash I see about things that aren't "really" Steampunk comes either from absolute beginners sussing things out, or from people who have been fans for a long time. They have been LARPing, writing, creating, reading, attending cons, dressing up, and spending their time and energy on something the love for a long time. They see their beloved idea being infiltrated and changed by the newcomers. But...

Making it to the party early doesn't make it your party.

In fact, hosting a party doesn't even make it your party, as many an event planner will tell you. The party, or in this case the Steampunk scene, cannot help but be shaped by those guests who come later, who come with a different set of experiences or skills, who want to join in the conversation even when others are mid-sentence. These newcomers should not only be allowed in, but welcomed with open arms.

There are two ways to deal with a difference of opinion: "No, but" and "Yes, and." The first is how most people respond, especially if something they believe is being challenged. They circle their mental wagons and create arguments to justify their own sense of self (though of course we aren't aware that this is why, we think of it as "truth") and let the bullets fly. They do battle with their enemy and try to vanquish them with words.

What if instead we acknowledge the other person's point of view, find a common ground (Yes) and then continue the conversation in a constructive way (and)? Humans love to draw lines between things, but couldn't we just keep moving the line and widening the circle?

What Does "Meaning" Even Mean?

Of course, there are some facts that are immutable. Gravity works whether or not you believe in it. The energy of the sun powers our world. But can you say with certainty that the sun rises in the east? Most accurately, the sun appears to rise in the direction commonly agreed upon by the majority of human beings to be called "east" (or one of its counterparts in another language).

We believe that there is an "east" because we need a way to bring order to our world and communicate with others, but that doesn't actually make east a "real" thing. Most other animals use detectable magnetic field lines to navigate, not some imaginary arrow superimposed on a map by us uppity primates. Birds only fly south for the winter because we say they do. In their own minds, they are simply going where they need to go.

Steampunk is *not* an immutable fact. It is an idea. Further, it is an idea based on punking the status quo, and striving to innovate and express themselves however we are able. Telling a person their voice is not welcome is the opposite of the movement that bore Steampunk in the first place.

However, the circle can't expand forever. There does need to be some kind of limit imposed on a word or it ceases to have meaning at all. For instance, the recent Brendan Fraser film *Journey to the Center of the Earth* is not a straight retelling of Jules Verne's book by the same name. In short, the original work hails from the steam era and it definitely gets "punked."

Does that make it Steampunk? In this case, I personally don't think so. It utterly lacks the aesthetic quality inherent in Steampunk, and it goes so far off-script from the original, I'd say it's more accurately classified a re-imagining or homage than an adaptation. Would it be appropriate to berate someone for claiming it is Steampunk? No. Do I think Steampunk fans could find something to like about it and connect with? Yes. So, if we're having a good time, how important is it that we agree?

On the flip side, I encourage anyone who has ever been told something of theirs or something they posted or loved "isn't Steampunk" to stand up for your right to add to discussion with this phrase:

Making it to the party early doesn't make it your party.

This doesn't mean I forgot about you beautiful weirdos who have been here all along, but if we want to see Steampunk flourish, we're all going to have to share the sandbox. If I haven't convinced you yet, I doubt I ever will. So just take a deep breath, close your eyes, and focus on all the cool toys the new kids might bring to the playground when they arrive.

A Few Parting Thoughts

If you've reached this point by reading straight through the book, you have now meandered through seven years of my ramblings and recommendations when it comes to Steampunk as a genre and aesthetic. Hopefully, you'll be leaving with some fun new ideas for bringing a little steam into your life. In this final segment, I want to talk about bringing some of your life into the steam.

Many people find Steampunk intimidating when they first encounter it. They see the quality of other people's costumes and props, the beauty of the models, the amount of time and effort that goes into a creation or performance, and are left with a feeling of "How can I ever measure up? How can I ever fit in?" Maybe it's a lack of skill, maybe it's a lack of money. Or maybe, it's simply a lack of confidence.

Here's the wonderful thing about Steampunk. There is *no right or wrong way to do it.*

Don't sew? So, what? If you do like to do *any* type of craft, I guarantee there's a way to put a Steampunk spin on it. I like to work with paper and mixed media collages. I've seen Steampunk sculptures, dolls and doll houses, vampire hunting kits, furniture, working dirigibles, teapot racers, parasols, computer mods, props of all shapes and sizes, paintings, drawings—you name it! Any medium can be bent to a Steampunk's will.

Can't string two sentences of fiction together? No biggie. Being a reader rather than a writer is a great way to be a part of the scene. Support authors by buying their books, leaving reviews, and sharing your thoughts with other fans.

Too shy for the spotlight? There are plenty of people who are happy to step into it for you. Buying albums or being out in the audience, cheering others on is just as vital to keeping the music coming as picking up an instrument yourself.

Tall? Short? Skinny? Fat? Dark? Light? There is a character or costume out there for you if you want it.

There's room for all kinds of participants.

Personally, I love going to conventions in order to listen to lectures, and I give some in return. If no one came to my talks, I wouldn't keep doing it. But there is clearly an audience for the history side of things as well as the other aspects.

And when it comes to dressing up, it is fun, but not a requirement. I have health problems that prevent me from wearing a corset and sometimes I "muggle" my way through an event in my regular clothes because I just don't feel well enough to put in the extra effort. I have never once felt unwelcome no matter what I am wearing. Even though making and donning elaborate costumes is the highlight of Steampunk for some people, I have never once met someone who is nasty to someone just because they aren't dressed up.

Recently, I've also seen an increasing number of people showing up with adapted braces, wheelchairs, and scooters. Parents with little kids will decorate their strollers or backpacks, and many events offer a kid-friendly programming track so families can enjoy the festivities together. Heck, some people even bring their pets along for the ride!

Although you may never go to a convention or meetup in person, I hope you find people to connect with on the Internet. There are forums and Facebook groups, Pinterest boards, and websites that especially cater to loving this fandom of ours. Even if you didn't connect with some of what I included in this book, there is something out there for everyone. You just have to find it.

So, go forth my friends, and make Steampunk whatever it is you want it to be.

I can't wait to see what you do.

Read More From Phoebe Darqueling: Riftmaker

Save his boy, uncover a conspiracy, and master opposable thumbs—a dog's work is never done.

Buddy's favorite thing is curling up for a nap at the foot of Ethan's bed. Then he stumbles through a portal to a clockwork city plagued by chimeras, and everything changes... Well, not everything. Sure, his new human body comes with magic powers, but he'd still rather nap than face the people of Excelsior, who harbor both desire and fear when it comes to "the other side."

He discovers Ethan followed him through the portal and

underwent his own transformation, and it becomes Buddy's doggone duty to save him. Buddy finds unlikely allies in an aristocrat with everything on the line, a mechanic with something to hide, and a musician willing to do anything to protect her. Using a ramshackle flying machine, the group follows the chimeras deep into the forest and uncovers a plot that could reshape the worlds on both sides of the rift.

Find this book in electronic and print formats at www.bit.ly/Riftmaker

Read More from Phoebe Darqueling: Mistress of None Series

Other people just think they're "haunted by the past." In Vi's case, it's true.

Clairvoyant Viola Thorne wants to forget about her days of grifting and running errands for ghosts. The problem? Playing it safe is dull. So when a dead stranger begs for her help, she jumps at the chance to dust off her hustling skills. The unlikely companions are soon tangling with bandits, cheating at cards, and loving every minute.

Then she finds out who referred him, and Vi has to face both a past and ex-partner that refuse to stay buried. Though she betrayed Peter, his spirit warns her of the plot that cost him his life. Vi's guilty conscience won't let her rest until she solves his murder. Though she's spent her whole life fighting the pull of the paranormal, it holds the key to atoning for the only deception she's ever regretted—breaking Peter's heart.

No Rest for the Wicked is available from in e-book, print, and audio formats. Find them all at www.bit.ly/ViolaThorne

Nothing Ventured, Nothing Gained: Mistress of None Book 2 hits shelves August 2020.

Edited by Phoebe Darqueling

24 international authors have come together to create this pair of anthologies for Steampunk lovers. The stories range from light and comedic to dark and full of drama, so fans of the genre both old and new are bound to find something they love within these pages.

What will you find in Cogs, Crowns, and Carriages?

Secrets and Airships - An airship pirate's daughter schemes to escape the reach of her father and discover a long lost treasure.

EDITED BY PHOEBE DARQUELING

By A. F. Stewart

Regicide and Prejudice - An unexpected inventor has the chance to prove his mettle when he is asked to protect Prince George from assassins. By Paul Michael

Gho-Power - A steam carriage designer harnesses an unusual new energy source with surprising consequences. By Michael Chandos

Nihon Daitan'na - The Americans will stop at nothing to force Japan to open its borders, but they can't predict what the Emperor has in store for them. By TJ O'Hare

Monster of the Deep - A steamship signals for help, but when it arrives, the crew has disappeared without a trace. By Thomas Roggenbuck

Where the Light Enters - An apprentice's loyalty is tested when an inventor's young wife looks to him for an escape from her loveless marriage. By Crysta K. Coburn

Treason in the Sky - A wartime mechanic discovers a wide-reaching conspiracy with ties to her and her forgotten past. By Jacy Sellers

Catchin' Gargoyles - A gargoyle hunter thinks he knows everything about them until his latest mission proves him wrong. By Tim Kidwell

The Last Sleep - A post-mortem photographer wishes to save her brother from his illness, but she learns everything comes with a price. By Sarah Van Goethem

The Mobius Trip - a shapeshifter's psyche is shattered by the asylum's experiments and he's doomed to repeat the same delusion-filled hour. By Phoebe Darqueling

The Last Automaton of Doctor Jubal Varva - An aging inventor builds one last machine to end the decades-long war and atone for past mistakes. By KA Lindstrom

Peregrine Rising: A Skies of Fire and Lightning Story - A sky pirate is pressed into service to recover a stolen item from an old nemesis. By Drew Carmody

What will you find in Gears, Ghouls, and Gauges?

The Mechanist's Daughter - When a little girl and her malfunctioning automaton show up on her doorstep, an inventor must solve the mystery of its origin. By Tracie McBride

The Lady Defiance - A harpy is taken captive and finds unexpected allies among the crew of airship pirates who liberate her. By Mandy Burkhead

An Evening on Harbor Ridge - Three soldiers must navigate a no man's land of steam-powered weapons and vampiric aristocrats to return home. By Mark Rivett

In the Cavern of the Sleepers - Asif's search for a cure for his narcolepsy leads him to a temple hidden in the Assam jungle where gods are stirring. By Ali Abbas

Fractured Moonlight - A pilot confronts his deceased father's best friend in his pursuit of understanding the events of the past. By W. T. Paterson

Basic Black - With a dreaded illness hanging over their heads, an engineer must decide what she is willing to sacrifice to protect her family. By K.A. Fox

The Grand Assault - A boy must step in to an unusual fencing match when the original challenger becomes embroiled in a conspiracy. By J. Woolston Carr

The Steam Horses of Stem Park - In a faraway future, sentient animals find inspiration in the Steampunk tales of the past. By Robert B. Read Jr.

Jewels from the Deep, a Sussex Steampunk Tale - A top London criminal visits the coast to assess local smugglers but more than potential profits are waiting for him beneath the waves. By Nils Nisse Visser

The Bronze Bomber - In the world of an alternative American Civil War, new inventions have shifted the tide and a Union agent seeks revenge. By Briant Laslo

La Muerda - A space western where a hard-bitten woman tries to learn the fate of her best friend on a planet known for debauchery and crime. By Mercury

Divine - A woman must ally herself with her murderous husband and a bigoted airship captain if she has any hope of discovering her true inheritance. By E. A. Catania

About the Illustrator

In addition to his graphic design work, P. R. Chase is an author of Steampunk-themed erotica, with two short stories appearing in two separate anthologies from House of Erotica Books, *Valves and Vixens 3* and *A Dose of Murder, Mystery, and Mayhem.*

His writing and love of the Steampunk genre, however, extends beyond erotica. He is one of the two contributing authors to an epistolary-format Victorian-age adventure Web fiction novel called Rackham and Crane, available on a shared blog at www.the-epistolary.org/rackhamandcrane/.

In addition to the Steampunk- and Victorian-themed erotica, P. R. Chase also has launched a series of modern-day erotica short stories, also available in e-book format.

www.ingramcontent.com/pod-product-compliance
Lightning Source LLC
Chambersburg PA
CBHW031107080526
44587CB00011B/864